THE HAPPY LAWYER

How to Gain More Satisfaction,
Suffer Less Stress,
and Enjoy Higher Earnings
in Your Law Practice

by

Larry Schreiter

Shiloh Publications

THE HAPPY LAWYER

How to Gain More Satisfaction,
Suffer Less Stress, and Enjoy Higher Earnings
in Your Law Practice

by
Larry Schreiter

Shiloh Publications
24909 104th Ave. SE., Suite 204
Kent, WA 98031 U.S.A.
(253)850 1579
(253)850-1549 Fax

First Printing 1999
Cover design by Herson Design, Portland, OR

ISBN 0-9670165-0-9
Library of Congress Catalogue Card Number: 99-90137

To my dad,
with gratitude for all he taught me

Disclaimer

Great care has been taken to provide accurate and current information; however, the ideas, suggestions, principles and conclusions presented in this book are subject to local, state and federal laws and regulations, court precedents and state bar policy determinations. This material is not intended to be a substitute for thorough legal or accounting advice. The reader is urged to seek and obtain such advice regarding particular application of the principles and ideas presented in this material, as specific circumstances may indicate other or contrary approaches. Neither the author nor the publisher shall have any liability or responsibility to any person or entity with respect to any loss or damage caused, or alleged to be caused, directly or indirectly by the information contained in this book. **If you do not wish to be bound by the above, you may return this book to the publisher for a full refund.**

Table of Contents

About the Author

Larry Schreiter has practiced law since 1978. His experience includes civil and criminal trial practice, business, real estate and tax practice, and estate planning. He has worked as a government lawyer, and in private practice in a partnership, a firm, and as a sole practitioner.

His personal and professional journey has led him to adopt a unique approach to clients. Aspects of his approach have been profiled in *Lawyers Weekly USA* and the *ABA Journal.*

Larry started sharing his successful methods with other lawyers in 1997, with the audiotape & workbook program *Seven Keys to Fortune and Fulfillment in Your Law Practice*, in "teleclasses" for lawyers across North America. Larry wrote *The Happy Lawyer* to help lawyers like you to find that which is most important to you about the practice of law, and to show you how to create your own path to true personal and professional satisfaction in your own practice.

Acknowledgments

I want to thank all who contributed to the development of this book, including Dr. Tony Alessandra, Andrew Barber-Starkey, Jack Canfield, Dr. Lynda Falkenstein, Ronald W. Fox, Esq., Douglas D. Germann, Sr., Esq., Michael Jeffreys, David Maister, Dr. Julie Miller, and David Ward, Esq. And I gratefully acknowledge the following sources:

Communicating at Work © 1993, by Dr. Tony Alessandra, used with permission. For information about Dr. Alessandra's books, audios or videos, visit http://www.alessandra.com, or call (619) 459-4515 or FAX (619) 459-0106.

True Professionalism: The Courage to Care About Your People, Your Clients, and Your Career, (Free Press, 1997), by David H. Maister, used with permission. Contact Maister Associates, Inc., (617) 262-5968 or FAX (617) 262-7907, E-mail David_Maister@msn.com, or visit http://www.davidmaister.com.

Referral Magic: The Complete Guide to Attracting New Clients and Developing a Successful Law Practice! © 1997, by David M. Ward, used with permission. Telephone (800)361-4724, FAX (949) 888-6488, E-mail davidward@home.com, or visit http://davidward.com.

Introduction

*Unhappiness is in not knowing what we want
and killing ourselves to get it.* — *Don Herold*

The holiday music tape came to an end. I paused in my writing to flip the cassette. It was the weekend before Christmas and everyone else in the firm was out preparing for the holidays. But I was at the office pounding out another trial brief.

Come the first of the year, I faced an appellate argument and several lengthy trials and arbitration hearings, all back to back. The pressure had been on all fall, with one matter after another coming up for trial or hearing. There was no let up in sight. And I was feeling sorry for myself.

My dedication to my clients is typical of thousands of hard-working lawyers in all areas of practice, all over the country. That kind of dedication had led me, in that instance, to forego family and friends, the holidays themselves, in order to do my professional best. I believe I am not at all unusual.

Control of Time, and Freedom to Decide

Yet how different this appeared from how I'd lived between college and law school. Back then, I had lived in a big-city fourth-floor walkup, painted with acrylics, wrote poetry, made jewelry, and rode my motorcycle. The rest of my time I spent in *really* frivolous self-indulgence! Work was something done just often enough to pay the bills!

What had been my ideal in that lifestyle? *Control of my own time and the freedom to decide what the shape of each day would be.*

Even when I started law school, as different as that was from the easygoing lifestyle I had been used to, my ultimate vision was the same: ***I could practice wherever and whenever I chose.***

But years later, I realized that depressing holiday season had crystallized for me the reality that I had gradually, incrementally, betrayed my own vision of a life in the law. I had come to feel intense dissatisfaction, resulting from my time not being my own. I had become angry and resentful. I had allowed myself to lose control to someone else's version of what makes up a life practicing law.

What Does Your Life in the Law Look Like?

Maybe you recognize this picture?

✓   Long energy-exhausting hours?

✓   Demanding clients?

✓   Crushing workloads leaving little or no free time for self, loved ones or recreation?

✓   Reluctance or guilt about taking vacations for fear of lost income and opportunities?

You are not alone.

Misery in the Legal Profession

Evidence suggests that there exists a large population within the legal profession who are in a state of misery.

✓   America has nearly one million lawyers at work,

and more on the way.

✓ One of three lawyers reports being dissatisfied with his or her working life.

✓ A majority complain of too little time for themselves or their families.

✓ Lawyers are four times as likely as the general population to suffer from depression, *the highest incidence found among 105 occupations.*

✓ Out of all the clients they work for or the matters they work on, lawyers reportedly either *dislike* or *barely tolerate* some 70% to 80%.

✓ Sole practitioners wonder where the next engagement will come from, find that time off comes at the price of an interruption of income, and are among the least satisfied.

Sound familiar to you? Can you relate any of these observations to your own situation? Do not despair. You can change it.

Then and Now

I experienced all of those frustrations back then, and that is how I felt back then. But now, I rejoice at the free time I enjoy, the control I have regained, and the dramatic improvements in both my life and my practice. All the result of my making certain very deliberate choices and changes.

My narrowly focused sole practice pays the bills and then some. I have clients I love working with. Many of them actually smile as they pay my fees. They attest to the value of what I provide them. To me, this brings great satisfaction.

Looking back, I see that the new year did come and go, much as the previous ones had. I cannot even remember what those cases were, or how they came out. I do know that every time I hear that particular tape of Christmas music, I am reminded of my last sacrificed holiday season.

Looking back, I would say that I have gone from frustration to fulfillment, with a good bit of fortune along the way. I wrote this book to show you how to do what you need to do to enjoy the same dramatic success.

Your Questions, Your Answers, Your Possibilities

This book will take you step by step, posing the crucial questions that you and you alone must answer. I will show you what to do with your answers.

If you will take action, following the prescriptions and principles set forth in this book, you will learn to:

✓ find your unique resources for increasing satisfaction in the law practice

✓ identify what I call your *YES! Clients*

✓ revolutionize your use of time and reclaim it for yourself and your loved ones

✓ make powerful connections with clients

✓ propel growth in your earnings

Ask yourself: right now, do you have the time you want

for the people you love and the activities you care about? Or, are you crushed by the sheer weight of client demands, money pressures, complaints and self-pity?

Are you ready to make some changes? Would you like to create a picture of a better way to practice your profession? And then put into action the steps necessary to make that vision your reality? You can, with the help of *The Happy Lawyer*. And there is every reason to believe you will succeed.

Professional Satisfaction is a Lawyering Skill

The Happy Lawyer will completely change your perspective. Achieving satisfaction need not await some sort of utopian reform of the legal profession. You, the individual lawyer, can achieve satisfaction by choice, by rebuilding your life in your chosen profession. This shift in viewpoint will provide immediate benefits.

As Daniel Evans has written, *"Learning to see things differently can actually have at least three different benefits. It can eliminate the stress we experience and allow us to enjoy our professions. It can also remove a barrier to effective advocacy and counseling, making us better lawyers and allowing us to serve our clients better. For similar reasons, it can also help us manage our offices more effectively because it allows us to listen to our partners and employees and deal with their concerns without fear or anger."*

So let us embark on a journey together, one of discovery, of *"learning new ways of looking at what we do (or unlearning what we have been doing)."* Speaking from my experience, I believe that your quest to increase professional satisfaction will result in enormous personal growth.

Your Notes

Chapter One:
Discover the Seeds of Satisfaction in Your Law Practice

Success follows doing what you want to do. There is no other way to be successful. — Malcolm Forbes

Before you can begin on the road to your own greater professional satisfaction, are you certain what will bring "satisfaction" to you? If you are not certain, if it is a little vague, then how can you reasonably expect doing what you have always done will ever lead to your satisfaction?

If you were about to begin a journey into unfamiliar territory, would you not wish to have at least a road map on which to rely? To begin putting your road map together, let us start with some thoughtful examination of what may bring you satisfaction.

The Individual Quest for Satisfaction

Consider first some sources of satisfaction. How about the feeling of satisfaction that comes from some experience that gives you a sense of achievement? The achievement may be concrete, as in a job well done.

It may be an outcome that was attained only through the application of your highest skills. Or the achievement may be more abstract, such as one gradually gaining a reputation of prominence.

You can also derive satisfaction from the recognition of others. This might come from personal or professional engagements, or perhaps from some other noteworthy endeavor, like chairing a charity fund drive, becoming part of a laudable organization or effort, receiving recognition for pro bono work.

Sometimes you may feel satisfaction in the gratitude of others. When a client expresses genuine appreciation for your efforts, do you allow yourself to receive those expressions with a sense of satisfaction? Receiving the thanks of others can bring deep satisfaction, even in trying times.

Just finding a state of contentment can be immensely satisfying. Feet up, relaxed, soft music, a sunset, or whatever setting you might conjure up in your mind as a picture of pure contentment, such a scene is suffused with sense of pure satisfaction. Being in the company of good friends, companions who are accepting and undemanding of you adds to the scene. Engaging in leisure activities for enjoyment and pleasure brings additional satisfaction.

Another source of satisfaction is your own fulfillment, your own feeling of reaching towards your potential. Maslow's famous "hierarchy of needs" places self-actualization at the height of human developmental needs, even higher than esteem and recognition.

In my view, consciously moving towards personal fulfillment through meaningful achievement in the practice of law results in greater professional satisfaction. Feeling that I have accomplished something that moves me in the direction of my highest aspirations is the very wellspring of fulfillment for me.

My own orientation then is achievement in combination with fulfillment. This is something I have come to through long and sometimes painful experience.

At the outset, both before and after my fourth-floor walk-up period, I was the typical over-achiever, with the paper credentials to prove it. As I entered the law, however, I soon found that mere achievement was not enough.

My dissatisfaction had me thinking it was time to abandon the law. Yet, as I began to confront my own desire for change, it appeared to be more a need to search for higher aspirations, to serve a set of deeper values. This in turn led to a new sense of purpose. For me, fulfillment comes from achieving progress towards a set of goals in furtherance of higher purpose.

What satisfaction means and where it will ultimately come from may vary widely from individual to individual. It may be something that only you can discover for yourself.

What we all have in common, however, is how satisfaction relates to our values. What has research in the legal profession shown?

The Legal Profession and Fundamental Values

Research on professional development across the spectrum of the entire legal profession has articulated four "fundamental values." When you consider the implication of these values, you will see why I maintain that the seeds of satisfaction are to be found in your law practice. These values directly support the notion of self-realization within the framework of your work as a lawyer. Let us consider what these fundamental values are.

As lawyers, we have obligations that relate to our clients, our society, our legal profession, and ourselves. The most well-known research into professional development of lawyers postulated four fundamental values of the legal profession. The four values are:

1. the obligation to learn to represent clients competently

2. the obligation to promote justice, morality and fairness

3. the obligation to improve the profession, and

4. the obligation continually to improve and employ one's skills in circumstances consistent with one's personal values and professional goals.

This last value is the one which most concerns us:

"To employ one's skills in circumstances consistent with one's personal values and professional goals."

How might this value help us to move towards greater satisfaction? In my view, professional development must mean more than mere continuing legal education to keep up-to-date technically.

The Happy Lawyer strikes a balance between developing technical skills and aligning them with well thought-out personal values and professional aspirations.

To the extent that we fail to improve our technical skills, we may fail to serve our clients, our profession and our society.

To the extent that we fail to employ our skills in positions consistent with our personal values and professional goals, we fail ourselves.

Clearly, there exists more than one way, one method, one path to follow. Indeed, these four fundamental values go a long way to explain why different lawyers derive satisfaction from so many divergent circumstances and styles of practice. Some thrive on high profile and controversial cases of notoriety.

A Litigator at the Crossroads

One such lawyer is Gerry Spence. The well known author of best selling books as well as a highly regarded speaker and commentator on the legal scene, Spence's life in the law was once far from what it has become. The path he took is illuminating.

Long before his name gained national exposure, Gerry Spence was a workaday trial lawyer. He accomplished good outcomes for his clients, indeed, some remarkable achievements.

But along the way, Gerry Spence came to the realization that he was employing his skills and talents in a way that did not mesh with his personal values. He had come to feel that it was no longer acceptable for him to represent corporations. It was not that he became opposed to corporations having legal representation, just that he was uncomfortable representing them. He was at a crossroads.

After much soul-searching, he announced his decision to his law partner: he intended to re-orient his law practice to serve only individuals.

Thus, Gerry Spence began on the path of aligning his professional activities with his personal, deeply held values. Since then, he has represented clients across the entire American political and socio-economic spectrum, from white separatist Randy Weaver to the Philippines' deposed and exiled first lady, Imelda Marcos.

But, he writes, the thread running through representing people over his career has been his abiding commitment to achieve justice for all his clients.

Satisfaction In Dissimilar Circumstances

Very few lawyers tread similar paths under the spotlight of the national media. Yet it remains true that what is fulfilling, rewarding and enjoyable to one would be a miserable curse to another. And the joy of it is that within the legal profession, there is room for all of us to express our deeply held values in our work.

It does not matter whether you are a matrimonial lawyer dealing with the merits of a delicate and divisive issue in a case, a tax lawyer toiling in obscurity on behalf of a harried taxpayer, or a criminal defense lawyer trying to summon up in the jury the courage to look a reasonable doubt squarely in the face.

If what you do in your professional life mismatches your deeply held values and goals, then you will not find satisfaction.

If, on the other hand, you mold your practice to align with those values and goals, the work will bring you satisfaction. Your work will propel you along to self-realization and you will enjoy a sense of doing your best while you move along the path to your own potential.

If you feel the practice of law results in too little time for yourself, occasionally frustrating dealings with clients, too many demands, deadlines, pressures and disappointments, or inadequate earnings for the time put in, then I suggest you look to ways to increase the focus on fulfillment. You ask, is this possible? I say definitely yes!

Your Self-Concept

It has long been known that our career choices subconsciously reflect our self-image. We each have made certain career choices which in some way serve to implement our own self-concept.

In my case, I can clearly identify certain experiences and choices that led me to the law. For example, when I was working as a sales clerk in a university book store, there was an effort to bring us into the white-collar union that already represented the university library's non-professionals. It seemed a natural extension of the union to organize those who worked in the university's bookstores. So an effort was mounted, and I found myself actively involved.

When the university resisted the effort, contesting the "appropriateness of the bargaining unit," the union's attorneys were called upon to argue the case. I found myself observing a National Labor Relations Board hearing on behalf of the bookstore employees.

As I listened to the presentation of the facts and argument of the legal principles, I found myself thinking, *I could do that*. (In fact, I found myself thinking I could do it better!)

Although I never again had any desire to work in labor law, I did find that experience to be critical in my decision to pursue a legal education a few years later. I was intrigued by the intellectual challenge in presenting the interests of others persuasively and forcefully.

Like me, you also had experiences that preceded the decision to undergo the rigors of getting a legal education and entering a competitive, stressful occupation. Yet how you have processed and internalized these experiences relates to your sense of who you are. Let us begin exploring some of these experiences.

A Word about the *Happy Lawyer* Exercises

Throughout the book, you will find Exercises. If the subject matter of a particular Exercise does not appeal to you at the time, skip over the Exercise and come back later. You are the one looking for answers, and each Exercise is designed to illuminate for you the matters under consideration. To do each Exercise, you will need at least one sheet of paper. Or you might do what some of my teleclass participants have found useful, and keep a notebook handy, so you have a convenient place to write down your responses and reactions as you read or do the Exercises. And the Appendix reproduces twelve of the Exercises as Worksheets.

The Exercises in this Chapter are here to help you begin to contemplate how the person you were before entering law has been changed by practicing. To learn and articulate where you are receiving satisfaction, and where you are not. The Exercises are designed to help you identify in writing the insights you gain when you consciously focus on these issues. So in getting started, it will be helpful to take a look back at what led you to choose a career in the law.

Exercise in Remembering

Summary:
Travel back in time. Gather impressions of your early experiences and influences that led you to choose the law.

Steps:

1.   Put aside for a moment the concerns of the present day, and let your mind relax.

2.   Read each of the following, close your eyes, and call to mind whatever images, feelings, memories, people, situations, each one evokes.

3. After a few moments' reflection on each one, jot down a note or two.

4. What was the earliest occasion you recall when you thought of becoming a lawyer?

5. What particular person, event, or cause was involved?

6. What alternatives were also under consideration?

7. What factors led you to choose the path you did?

8. During law school or at any time since, if you have ever thought of quitting, remember that time of doubt, and call to mind the considerations that you were weighing at that time. What were they?

9. You have remained with the law. Why?

10. Jot down as many words or phrases that relate to the factors that influenced you to stick with it.

✓*Points to Ponder:*

What was the earliest occasion you wrote about? Did it involve:

- a person? an event? a cause?

- What connection exists between your recalled person, event or cause and what you do now in your law practice?

- How is what you do now like what you recalled?

- How is it different?

- Did you *outgrow* what you recalled? Did it *just fade* into the past?

- Would the thought of moving towards what you recalled feel in some sense like *progress*? Or *regression*?

- What value or skill does what you recalled represent to you?

- What useful or thought-provoking comparison can you make between your initial stimulus towards a legal career and how you now feel about what it has been like to practice?

- How has this Exercise helped you to pinpoint your specific sources of dissatisfaction?

- Are there apparent sources such as relentless pressures, a need to increase billable hours, and loss of control?

- Are there deeper feelings of resentment or a sense of disconnection from your own fundamental values?

Now, let us look at what is different about legal work from what you did before the law. This next Exercise is compares your work before entering the law, how work has changed, and how you have changed.

Exercise in Work Before the Law

Summary:
Looking at pre-law involvement in the world of work.

Steps:

1. Call to mind all your work experiences, volunteer positions, summer jobs, or other employment completed before entering law.

2. Of those that had any bearing on your career choice, jot down the images, feelings, or memories that they invoke.

3. List all the skills you employed in these positions, and any key talents you possessed that were either key to your success or were left unused.

✓ *Points to Ponder*

• What link is there between your responses, and what you are doing now in the law?

• What value or skill does this relate to?

• How is what you do like that earlier experience or position?

• Comparing your attorney experiences to these earlier experiences, is it positive? Or something else?

• Would moving towards use of the talents or skills employed then seem to you to represent *progress*? Or *regression*?

Now that you have begun to explore the distance between your initial images and the reality, it may help to forge a new vision, a renewed image, to spend some time drawing upon your earlier figures of emulation.

Looking *Into*, Rather Than Up to, Your Heroes

Who our heroes are reveals a lot about the qualities and characteristics we admire in others, and probably would like to emulate ourselves. It is useful, not so much to look *up* to our heroes, as to look *into* them.

Our heroes may be members of our own families, or drawn from the larger community, historical or contemporary.

What inspiration can you draw from the lives of your heroes in order to nourish your vision?

Benefits to be gained are insights into unfulfilled aspirations, aspects and values you feel drawn to, and lighting up aspects that you may be putting to good use now in your practice, at least some of the time.

Even more revealing, it can illumine aspects that would benefit you if employed more fully in your practice.

You would increase satisfaction from a practice that allows you to express qualities you find worthy of admiration in your heroes.

A lawyer in one of my teleclasses on improving satisfaction found this Exercise particularly revealing. He realized that his primary hero had been his own father, whom he had admired for the ethical way he had conducted his business. His father had cared deeply for both customers and employees. This lawyer came to realize that in practicing law, he had let the rough and tumble of divorce and other contentious litigation obliterate that kind of devotion. And now he wanted to get it back.

To what attributes of your heroes do you aspire? Grit and determination? Quiet courage in taking the right stand, though showered with disapproval? Here is an Exercise to help you explore these issues.

Exercise Recalling Heroes

Summary:
Nourish your vision with inspiration from the qualities of your heroes.

Steps:

1. Think about those people whom you'd call your heroes.

2. Come up with three heroes. They may be known to you personally, now or in the past, or they may be historical figures, or familial ancestors.

3. For each of the three heroes you named, write whatever phrases or words capture whatever characteristic or quality makes this person a hero to you. Here is a list of traits or characteristics to aid you with your heroes:

Adventurous, Articulate, Brave, Competent, Conscientious, Creative, Curious, Decisive, Devoted, Disciplined, Effective, Eloquent, Enterprising, Expressive, Forgiving, Giving, Generous, Genuine, Gracious, Healthy, Honest, Inspirational, Inventive, Knowledgeable, Likable, Loyal, Magnetic, Modest, Motivated, Noble, Obedient, Persevering, Principled, Quiet, Reliable, Responsible, Self-sacrificing, Sensitive, Stalwart, Thorough, Trustworthy, Uplifting, Visionary, Willing, Worthy.

4. Write down the three primary traits or characteristics that stand out and towards which you feel a pull.

✓ *Points to Ponder*

•   What have you learned from looking at your heroes?

•   To what extent are the qualities you identified in this Exercise present in your law practice?

•   How much of your dissatisfaction is related to a discontinuity between your most admired values as reflected in others you admire, and your actual daily practice?

Let us now turn to a consideration of how you came to be in this situation.

Your Turning Points

How did you find yourself so far away from those traits to which you aspire? Have you ever wondered about the turning points in your life? Wondered, had those steps not been taken, had those decisions not been made, what your life would look like now?

Buried beneath what you are doing and not doing now, are markers of what you would most like to be doing. In the past, you will find the bedrock of a more fulfilling future.

None of us is the same person we were when we started law school or first went into practice. Yet our deepest sources of satisfaction can be explored in the context of our work, for they lie, like dormant seeds awaiting their germination and your cultivation.

Let us turn to the area of unfulfilled aspirations that lie, little changed, beneath the surface. Examining unacknowledged and unfulfilled aspirations and the obstacles blocking their expression can yield useful seeds of satisfaction. Use the Exercise to tap your memory for raw materials.

Exercise on Aspirations

Summary:
Remember earlier aspirations and state obstacles to their fulfillment.

Steps:

Complete the following sentences:

1. Before finishing high school, my most exciting daydream about my future was:

2. My favorite paid jobs before entering law were:

3. When I started law school, I saw the future as:

4. If I had all the financial security I need and I knew I could not fail, I think the way I would spend most of my time would be:

✓ *Points to Ponder:*

- To what extent do you feel that your legal work leads in the direction of your earlier aspirations?

- How have your experiences in the law modified your aspirations?

- Would movement towards your former aspirations feel in some sense like *progress?* Or *regression?*

- Is your legal career in line with your aspirations?

Let us now look into this question of alignment a little more deeply. We know that misalignment causes distress. A misalignment, if left denied, can lead attorneys to emotional distress, substance abuse, poor health, and a desire to run away from the law. But do not lose heart.

The great American psychologist, Karl Menninger, said that "Unrest of spirit is a mark of life." Your very dissatisfaction is the key to your renewal. The fact that you are reading this means you want something better.

The fact that you have not abandoned your legal career implies there are some seeds of satisfaction lying dormant beneath your daily activities.

Digging for Seeds of Satisfaction

It takes work to explore the potential for satisfaction concealed within your law practice. You have to dig out those parts that are deeply satisfying, and that are compatible with your values. Some of those will be reflected in the way in which you become engrossed in them. Let us consider those next.

All of us have experienced situations where our involvement in an activity was so total, that we have lost track of time. Research shows that at such times, what we are doing completely occupies all of our mind and awareness. Loss of self in an engrossing and enjoyable activity is often a sign of a child-like involvement akin to play. Researchers call such a state of mind "being in the flow."

This next Exercise lets you note activities you have encountered in your legal work where you have lost yourself, where you have been led into being in the flow.

Exercise on Being in The "Flow"

Summary:
Recall some experiences of that active state in which your absorption was so total that you forgot about the time.

Steps:

1. Sit quietly for a moment. Close your eyes if it helps you to concentrate.

2. Bring to mind a picture of yourself engaged in your practice. You may be in your office, in court, at a client's, or elsewhere. See yourself in your mind's eye so engaged.

3. Note what you are doing. Are you standing or sitting? Talking or listening? Writing or reading?

4. Now bring to mind an instance you remember where you found that you had become so engrossed in your work, that you lost track of the time.

5. Note it down, specifying what you were doing during the "flow" experience.

6. Repeat for two or three more such experiences.

✓ *Points to Ponder:*

•   What are the three most absorbing activities in your practice?

•   What do you enjoy the most about each activity?

•   What are the specific skills you employ when you are in the "flow?"

Reviewing all the responses you have made to the Exercises so far, what has struck you the most? Were there some surprises, or have you just put into written form what you have been aware of for some time?

Next, let us place your individual reactions in the larger context of the entire legal profession.

Thinking Like a Lawyer

The legal profession attracts "tough-minded, bottom-line decision makers and conceptual complex problem solvers." Lawyers enjoy using language as a tool for verbal persuasion. Law is an occupation that highly prizes verbal acuity. But unlike expressive writing, argumentation has a desired outcome as its object. "Those emerging from law schools are debaters, not poets."

The intellects of all first-year law students are subjected to a pitiless and deliberate assault. Students embarking on a law career either rise to the challenge, or fall by the wayside. Finally, by the end of the first year, the light of understanding seems to go on in more and more heads. Then it is said each student is starting to "think like a lawyer."

And you have been doing that now for some considerable period of time! You have adapted to a belief system and an analytical method comprised of a bewildering array of principles and rules.

To your friends from your pre-law life, you are enmeshed in the convoluted and arcane. In practice, you daily employ your skills to manipulate principles and rules in order to accomplish specific objectives for your clients. How do your daily experiences and beliefs match up to the profession as a whole?

While law is pervasive in America, it is misunderstood, and we lawyers are resented. Not only is there a "disconnection" between our actual life in "doing law" from the clients who benefit, but there is a societal disconnection, as well. The public perceptions and stereotypes of lawyers are almost uniformly negative: Lawyers are uncaring, cold, greedy, and manipulative.

U.S. Supreme Court Chief Justice William Rehnquist has reportedly discontinued using lawyer jokes to open his speeches. Why? Because audiences of lawyers had not been amused, he reported, and audiences of non-lawyers had not realized they were jokes!

As lawyers, we have almost daily association with human pain and conflict in our work. Cases involving death, personal injury, criminal activity, divorce and other strife raises the challenge of maintaining rational detachment.

Just as in such stressful occupations as firefighting, law enforcement and emergency medicine, our endurance of such acute stress leads to its internalization. Thus, too many lawyers internalize their stress into their "lawyer persona." Thus masked, who they truly are underneath is lost. "This systematic avoidance of involvement may in fact be at the heart of the lawyer's dilemma." So, let us examine your own beliefs about lawyers and the profession.

Exercise on Your Beliefs About Lawyers

Summary:
Take a frank look at your attitudes towards lawyer stereotypes.

Steps:

Complete the sentences:

1. I believe certain negative stereotypes of lawyers are mostly ***true***, and those true negative stereotypes are that lawyers:

2. I believe certain negative stereotypes of lawyers are mostly ***false***, and those false negative stereotypes are that lawyers:

3. Three ***strongly positive things*** I can say about lawyers, in my experience, are:

✓ *Points to Ponder:*

•   Do you have a "lawyer persona?"

•   Do you hold mostly positive or mostly negative views of lawyers?

•   How has the inevitable stress of practicing law affected your relationships?

Now, it is time to go back and review all your responses to the Exercises so far. Have you re-discovered any aspects of yourself? How have your responses illuminated for you those areas of your practice that tie in to where you started? How close a match is there with what you were looking for when you first embarked on a legal career?

Where are the breakdowns, the disconnects between those early aspirations and the realities of your practice? With these as your starting point, you can make improvements. Several factors should cheer the heart of every lawyer looking to improve the level of satisfaction.

Why You Should Be an Optimist

As a professional, you have the skills to create value by delivering results, outcomes, or representation to people who need your services. Yet unlike engineering or computer science, the benefits of achieving these objectives are rendered to clients who, as a rule, lack even the slightest idea that what we have done benefited them, or of how we have done it.

Therein lies an opportunity. If you significantly alter your client's perception of the value of results and your representation, you move yourself out of the category of "just another" lawyer, and into the category of "highly valued in the marketplace."

Second, you have the right of occupational self-determination. As a licensed professional, you can self-select from a host of practice specialties or concentrations, even in states where formal "specialist" designations are forbidden.

Third, you can take steps to bring your practice more into line with the fourth Fundamental Value of the profession: *to employ one's skills in circumstances consistent with your own personal values and professional goals.*

With the information from doing this Chapter's Exercises as your baseline, you can now begin to mine the really exciting part of your practice, those clients and matters that make you feel, "THIS is why I went to law school! This is what it is all about for me!"

I call them your ***YES! Clients.***

Your Notes

Chapter Two:
How to Choose *Your YES! Clients*

Don't let other people tell you what you want. — *Pat Riley*

Too many lawyers feel they must take whatever cases and clients come their way. Their practice careens and lurches along, often out of control. They fill their calendars with whoever and whatever happens to have come their way.

Like a stray dog at a professional whistlers' convention, they run here and there, confused and frantic, reacting to the latest demand or crisis presented by a client with a retainer check in hand. Does this resemble your situation?

One lawyer in my teleclasses on increasing satisfaction was astonished at the concept of choosing your clientele. It had simply never occurred to him, over 20 years in practice, that he was free to choose. Just the realization that much of his unhappiness stemmed from feeling overwhelmed by clients he disliked and their legal problems, and that he had the power to choose his way out, gave him a new sense of freedom. How about you? Start with this quiz.

Of All the Legal Work You Do,

What percent do you hate or strongly dislike? ____%

What percent do you find just tolerable? ____%

What percent is enjoyable or satisfying? ____%

Of All Your Clients,

What percent do you strongly dislike? ____%

What percent do you just tolerate? ____%

What percent do you actually like? ____%

How did you do? If you *hate or strongly dislike up to twenty percent* of your work, *just tolerate sixty to seventy percent,* and *find enjoyment and satisfaction in only twenty to twenty-five percent* of your work, you have a lot of company.

Is that tolerable? Is such an environment an acceptable place for you to spend the rest of your legal career? Do you want to do something about it? *Will* you do something about it?

Are you someone who makes things happen? If you want to make a change, I am going to suggest a simple, yet radical way to increase your level of satisfaction.

- Sort your clients and projects into those you enjoy, and those you do not.

- Analyze what it is that makes these clients and projects satisfying.

- Decide exactly what comprises your essential work.

- Decide to serve more clients work on more projects like those, within your definition of your essential work.

- Focus your practice, and decline whatever falls outside that focus.

This approach leads more quickly to an increased level of satisfaction than anything else, and it is not as difficult to achieve as it may seem at first.

Your Daily Balance of Satisfaction

When you get your bank statement every month, there is a figure called the average daily balance. This fictional number gauges the overall level in your account, smoothing out highs and lows in the account's activity by averaging.

Your life is like a bank account. Into your account there is a daily deposit, with no effort on your part, only here it is minutes instead of dollars. Each 24 hours consists of 1,440 minutes. You must consume that daily deposit, day after day. The only rule is that, at the end of the day, your balance will be zero.

There is no reason to spend the majority of your life just enduring either your work or your clients. But making the conscious choice to center your practice on legal work and clients similar to those that have been satisfying in the past is simply up to you.

With effort, vision and persistence, you can orient your practice to spend your days working on things that are exciting, that bring you satisfaction, and that provide real solutions to ideal clients. If a small portion fall in the "I really love this" category, then why not orient your practice around that?

This Chapter shows you how to raise your average daily balance of satisfaction by working more and more with your *YES! Client.*

Finding Your *YES!* Client

Do you have a *YES! Client*? Have you ever represented a client that you would brag about, if legal ethics allowed?

Do you have any clients whose calls you hasten to take because you enjoy every conversation or interaction with this client?

How about that client whose industry, problems or challenges present you with the opportunity to function at a peak level of professionalism? Or that client who gives you every evidence of genuinely appreciating your services? And do not overlook those who cheerfully pay your fees promptly!

We all have worked with a *YES! Client*. No matter how you came to work with any particular *YES! Client*, the client is one that, were it in your power, you would choose.

In other words, the ideal client. For each lawyer, your ideal client depends on who you are and what you can do for them better than anyone else. Your ideal client is your *YES! Client*.

If you are in private practice, then in fact you have probably already served a number of ideal clients. And you probably have worked on projects that you enjoyed, despite the client.

The clients and projects in your past offer you guidance on the way to discover your most satisfying work. You will easily call to mind one or two clients that fit this category. You may feel that coming up with any more will be an arduous process. I felt that way, too. But what I found is that if you think about what elements you enjoy, even in cases where the particular client was difficult, you can also uncover types of projects that bring you satisfaction.

Combining the two, you will find, offers a rewarding niche. So I urge you to take the time to uncover underlying factors that may contribute to your satisfaction in working with these clients. Here's how.

In his book, *True Professionalism: The Courage to Care About Your People, Your Clients, and Your Career,* David H. Maister suggests how to find the kinds of clients and work that bring satisfaction. He asks the lawyers in the firms using his consulting services to divide up their work and their clients into three categories:

• This I love, this is what I live for.

• This I tolerate, but it's a living.

• This I hate, I only do it because I get paid for it, but I'd rather be rid of it.

What makes up your *YES! Clients*? What are the projects that lead you to exclaim, *This* I love, *this* is what I live for? Some common characteristics include:

- Working for them serves your highest values.

- Providing the solution to their problem employs your greatest skill.

- The case appeals to you because you have relished similar cases in the past.

- Getting the opportunity to work in this kind of matter brings you enjoyment.

- The clients express appreciation for what you have to offer and value it with their checkbook.

As lawyers, we all have a professional responsibility to do our best for our clients. In the Exercises that follow, you will sort clients and their matters into different categories, and you are going to start to see some patterns emerge.

From the ideal client that you identify, you are going to make a "template."

Exercise to Discover Your *Yes! Clients*

Summary:
You already have served ideal clients. Now identify them.

Steps:

1. Gather together your past year or two years' client list, case list, pocket organizer and calendar, any other compilations that will assist you bring to mind those with whom you have been working.

2. Look over your list, and rank each entry. Assign "1" to clients you most enjoyed working with, "2" to those to whom you feel indifferent, and "3" to those you wish would go somewhere else.

3. Next, go over the results. For each client you ranked a "1" write down the particular issue or problem that you worked on and how you resolved it for them. Spell out in specific detail what the

problem was, what the work entailed and how your efforts provided a satisfying solution to the client's problem.

4.   Now pull out the nuggets. Look over the clients you have listed. For each one, reflect on what it was about that particular client that appealed to you. What were they like? What was their personality like? What was your working relationship like? What characteristics are recurring among those clients on your list? Jot them down.

5.   Now, how about the particular matters? Were there recurring kinds of issues, problems, or legal processes involved? Do some projects call upon your special strength in one or another field? What about the work strongly appeals to you? Jot those down.

6.   What skills and particular knowledge are you called upon to employ in addressing these problems? Note them down.

7. Now, review 1 through 6, and see if you spot certain values emerging, common themes, activities, skills, knowledge, in your favored clients, problems, projects, and solutions. List the common or overlapping themes.

✓ *Points to Ponder:*

• What are the kinds of clients and matters that bring you the most satisfaction?

• What is it about them that leads to that satisfaction?

• What profile has begun to emerge, of your most enjoyable and satisfying clients and matters?

Specifically considering their features and characteristics, you next want to pull all this together into a profile of your *YES! Clients.* That is, you are going to go from the specifics of that ideal client and their particular problem you so enjoyed working on to the generalized. In this way, you develop your template, your model of clients and matters from whom you have derived the greatest satisfaction.

Remember, you have the ability to determine whether you choose to work with any client or not. So, why not work with those who bring you satisfaction? Stringing together the highlights you have gleaned in the Exercises in this Chapter, you should be able now to formulate a composite of your ideal client and your ideal client matters.

Let's try it. From the foregoing, how would you now fill in the following?

"Taking into account my review of my clients over the recent period, I'd describe my YES! Client as one who:

"The kind of issue, problem, project or challenge I most favor their bringing to me I'd describe as:

"When I am working on this kind of matter for this kind of client, what I most enjoy about the relationship is:

"I like this because:

"The outcome produced these specific benefits:

"I receive the greatest reward from this because:

The Promise of Your Future Practice

Now you have brought into your focus those clients and matters which most positively motivate you. These engagements bring you the greatest enjoyment and satisfaction.

The profile of these *YES! Clients* and the characteristics of the work you most like doing for them are the seeds of satisfaction for your future practice.

Imagine for a moment what your life would be like, if you go forward from here and cultivate those seeds. If you build your future practice on this foundation. Working for those kinds of clients, on those kinds of matters.

Deliberately focusing on your *YES! Clients*, and their matters will lead you on the path to greater fulfillment and satisfaction. But to get there, you must control who becomes one of your clients. I refer to this process as staking out your *Arena of Preeminence.*

Your Notes

Chapter Three
Focus on Your *Arena of Preeminence*

To love what you do and to feel that it matters . . .
how could anything be more fun? — Katherine Graham

A law practice serving your *YES! Clients* promises the most satisfaction for you. Discerning the discrete aspects was the work of the previous Chapter. You went through the clients and matters, gathering those where you derived satisfaction and enjoyment, winnowing out the rest. You went on to spell out how your work benefited them, as well as how working with them on these projects used your highest skills and brought you the most rewards.

Now, the next step is to visualize a future practice that is devoted to greater emphasis on such engagements, for such clients on such projects. This greater focus in the areas you already know to be satisfying will enhance your sense of fulfillment and satisfaction in your law practice.

Establishing such a practice requires that you develop, articulate and deliver direct, powerful benefits to your *YES! Clients.* Benefits that only come to them through employing your services. Focusing everything you do around those benefits for those clients constitutes your *Arena of Preeminence.*

What Is Your *Arena of Preeminence?*

Your *Arena of Preeminence* provides the focal point for your reinvigorating practice. It comprises both the *YES! Clients* and the specific areas you have chosen. Those who qualify for inclusion in your *Arena of Preeminence* stand to reap the powerful benefits you have articulated. Within your *Arena of Preeminence,* you stand out from all the other attorneys in your market area. You dominate your *Arena of Preeminence.*

Your *Arena of Preeminence* contains *YES! Clients,* ideal matters and specific benefits intended for them. These are the objectives for your future practice. You must commit your practice to attaining those objectives. Your domination of your *Arena of Preeminence* depends directly upon your commitment to attaining and orchestrating all these objectives in your practice: *YES! Clients,* with special matters utilizing your special capabilities, so you can deliver powerful and valuable benefits.

Later Chapters address how to attract your *YES! Clients,* how to capitalize upon the depth and breadth of your specialized knowledge, experience and skills, and how to discern and communicate powerfully the solution or benefits to be provided. But first, you need to focus on your practice and see if you can identify several seeds, from which you might cultivate a more satisfying *Arena of Preeminence.*

To do this, first note down those aspects of your law practice that hold your interest. Whether it is the challenge of overcoming a difficult adversarial situation, or the satisfaction of skillful negotiation. The "aha!" of rooting out that key precedent, or the enjoyment of achieving some milestone. Whatever these may be, whatever aspects of your practice provide a lasting interest in your mind, note them down in the first part of this Exercise.

Next, note the skills and talents that you enjoy most utilizing in your practice. Try to capture the action, the activity, the talent that you like to employ.

Third, list what your intuition tells you are the three ways or areas where you might wish to expand, to give back, to grow.

These areas might be personal, professional, material, spiritual. Whatever, list them in the third section of this Exercise.

Exercise on *Arena of Preeminence*

Summary:
Identify a more satisfying *Arena of Preeminence*.

Steps:

Complete the following sentences.

1. Three aspects of my practice that really hold my interest are:

2. Three skills or talents used in my practice at which I excel are:

3. Three values of importance to me I would like my practice to serve are:

✓ *Points to Ponder:*

*   Explore what connections you might be able to make among these areas.

*   Match up each possible pair among the three Aspects, three Skills, and three Values you were asked for above.

*   Contemplate each match, asking yourself what relationship each may represent. What sort of connection occurs to you? How might each pair relate?

- As you align each matched pair, write down a word, a phrase, or more, that will stand for the relationship or connection that occurs to you.

- Among all the connections and relationships, which two or three strike you the most?

- Imagine you were to focus more on each of those striking aspects in your daily practice of law. Write down which you would choose to concentrate upon.

Those aspects point towards a more satisfying *Arena of Preeminence.* Commit to taking steps to place a greater emphasis on this a part of your practice in the next thirty days. It will help you to eliminate distractions and multiply opportunities. The next step is to examine how the purpose relates to your *YES! Clients.*

You want to start by putting your *Practice Purpose* into a single sentence or two.

Here is an example. Suppose in the earlier Chapters, you have decided that your ideal clients are reasonably sympathetic, cooperative people who have suffered personal injuries. Your own education, special knowledge and skills ideally prepare you to obtain good solid settlements and verdicts. And that in addition to financial rewards, you find working with these kinds of clients to achieve these ends very fulfilling.

Through the Exercises, you have confirmed that the skills of analyzing, empathizing and negotiating combine with the values of working to assist those who might otherwise become victims of the insurance system. This brings about aspects you really enjoy, particularly in putting together the settlement packages and negotiating settlements with the insurance company representatives. So, what is your *Practice Purpose?*

You might say "I am a personal injury lawyer." Okay, but that tells very little. You might instead say, "I represent injured persons, to recover for them compensation from those who have injured them."

That's better. But what if you had found that, instead of waiting for the big payoff and carrying all the huge outlay that big cases involve, that there is a real appeal in having a steady stream of recoveries from smaller, yet just as meritorious injury cases? This would offer several opportunities.

First, you could be more specific. You could say, "I aggressively seek full compensation for those with moderate to high damages from personal injury."

Second, you can hone in on your *Practice Purpose,* to differentiate yourself from all the other personal injury attorneys who all seem to be asking, for example in the yellow page ads, for only the big cases.

You could say, "My *Practice Purpose* is to bring to bear for those who, because of the negligence of others, have been injured to some real degree and have recoverable damages the very same level of experience, skill and aggressive representation as would be employed in representing a person with grievous injuries, so that even the modestly injured client with a meritorious case will have every chance to receive all the compensation to which our system of justice entitles them."

Now that is a focused purpose! Such a focus appeals not only to potential clients, but also to very powerful sources of referrals.

Note how this purpose focuses on a narrow market: those with demonstrable though modest personal injuries, bringing cases that others seem to overlook, belittle or handle only begrudgingly. It offers a unique niche that you can use to stake out as your own *Arena of Preeminence* and to market your practice.

Whatever your area of practice, this approach will illuminate your opportunity, and help you eliminate competition. Remember, no one else can offer exactly what you have to offer to your *YES! Client.*

Focus on your *Arena of Preeminence* . Your passion will engage people. They will know you care because they will feel it.

Here is an Exercise to help you round out your own *Practice Purpose* within your *Arena of Preeminence.*

Start with your ideal client's greatest worries or concerns, and consider how your special interests, skills, values and intuition all come together. Keep in mind the specific benefits that result to your client.

Exercise on *Practice Purpose*

Summary:
Base a *Practice Purpose* on benefits that result from applying your special interests, skills, values and intuition to solve your *YES! Client's* greatest concerns.

Steps:

Review your answers to Exercises in Chapters One and Two, and complete the following:

1. The solution or benefit I bring to my *YES! Clients* is:

2. The skills and knowledge I apply in doing so are:

3. The most satisfaction to me comes from:

4. To generalize from these experiences, I would conclude that my *Practice Purpose* is:

5. Stating that in a way that prospective clients would appreciate, I'd describe it as:

6. A law practice devoted to providing that benefit to such clients I would best describe this way:

Polishing Your Powers

Do you have everything you need to carry out this *Practice Purpose?* As you have drawn a clearer picture of your *YES! Client,* you have also called to mind the skills you employed in tackling their issues and problems. The special experience and knowledge that you have and can bring to bear to serve *YES! Clients* in the future uniquely qualify you to serve that client.

Once you decide on serving that population of *YES! Client* prospects, you will tailor the message of your practice to attract those clients into your office. Such intense concentration or specialization offers you an opportunity to earn higher fees, but to accomplish all this, you must become an expert. You may already be more of an expert than you realize. Practice helps us develop applied knowledge. And applied knowledge is needed each time we undertake a matter.

This next Exercise totes up your skills, knowledge and experience assets. Be sure to consider such applied knowledge in this Exercise. And be blunt about where you might be lacking, as well, so you might set about filling any gaps.

Exercise on Skills, Knowledge, Experience

Summary:
Recap your inventory of strengths.

Steps:

1. Review your educational background, including all areas studied, and those particularly suited to your ideal client.

2. Consider your knowledge of the industry, business practices or regulations that relate to your *Arena of Preeminence.* List additional areas of knowledge you need.

3. List practical experience and skills, as well as additional skills needed.

✓ *Points to Ponder:*

*   What skills, training or experience gives me the power to provide my *YES! Clients* the solutions they need?

*   What additional skills, training or knowledge do I need to obtain?

- What are the relevant organizations and affiliations that I have?

- To fill the gaps, gain additional skills, knowledge or affiliations, what are the actions I plan to take?

A *Practice Purpose* Is Ennobling

Your *Practice Purpose* will energize your highest aspirations to bring about the desired end results that benefit your *YES! Clients*. You are privileged to serve them with your services using your unique knowledge and specialization. Now you need to lay out your specific Plan to Take Control so you can overcome any and all obstacles.

Chapter Four:
Create Your Plan to Take Control

Never mistake motion for action. — *Ernest Hemingway*

Lawyers often complain of a trapped feeling, of their never having enough time. One attorney describes each work week as pushing a huge weight up a hill, only to have it roll back and crush over him as he ends the week in frustration, then starting all over again. What about you? Have you ever felt that your practice, its stresses and demands, had you out of control? How do you spend your time?

❏ Do you regard Saturdays, Sundays and weekdays after 5 PM as time to catch up?

❏ How do you feel about that?

Meet Joseph, Alicia, and Randall, three lawyers with very different practices. Their accounts illustrate the importance of having a plan to control your clients and their matters, control your interactions with others to deliver your services, and control of your own direction. As you read these accounts, think how each one might gain better control of their situation.

Joseph's Typical Day

Joseph has a busy general practice emphasizing criminal defense and bankruptcy in a Midwest big city.

This is an actual day, typical of several days every week. I start with four hearings all set at 9 am --all poorly paying court appointments. When I arrive, the families of all four defendants loudly denounce the police, the system, and me (for not having gone and seen their boys in jail). A full courtroom, prosecutors with files in buckets, and the jury box full of overnight arrests whose cases go first. I check my watch--how will I ever make it to my 11:30 am consultation, let alone the 10:30 am pretrial status conference?

My hearings finally get underway. One client refuses the offered plea and wants a trial. One has another charge pending that I didn't know about, and can't plead even though he wants to. The other two proceed without incident. I fill out the last plea form, and dash out, trailed by clients' family members, still complaining.

I speed to the other courthouse, arriving minutes before the pretrial status conference. Another full courtroom, my client listed eighty-seventh out of eighty-eight matters on the docket, and I have an office consultation in an hour. This judge generally refuses to take cases out of order. I smile and beg the clerk and bailiff to help me, and miraculously, they pull the file, and get the judge to take it after the on-duty officers' cases, greatly shortening the expected wait. The plea offered is a good one, in a case where a trial would be risky, but the client insists that I 'get him off.' Of course, he has not paid the second installment on my fee. So instead of waiting, I get the case continued, which just puts the conflict off two more weeks. Maybe he'll at least pay me by then.

I glance at my calendar, and realize that I'd forgotten about a meeting at 2 pm. Back at my office, I arrive to witness an irate client complaining to the receptionist about a garnishment that would not have happened if I had gotten her bankruptcy petition filed yet (true -- I just haven't had time!). My consultation clients are waiting. I spend nearly an hour with them, only to find out that they have absolutely no money to pay anything, and they leave without retaining me. I find out the receptionist forgot to collect the consultation fee.

No progress in the case comes out of the 2 pm meeting. Next I have consults, at 3 pm, 4 pm and 5:30 pm. Each one exhausts me more and more. At 6 pm, phone messages overflow my box and a pile of mail sits on my desk. I have messages to return, bankruptcy petitions to review and sign, and I haven't looked at the mail yet. When I do, I find four notices of court dates that will require continuances due to conflicts, and a stack of discovery in a case for which I have not been paid. I also have a note from my secretary reminding me to pay her health insurance premium.

I sign off the petitions without reading them, praying they are OK. I grab messages and start returning calls, only to reach voice mails. I put the phone down. The calendar shows that, rather than being able to catch up on anything tomorrow, I have a misdemeanor trial for a client who refused the plea offer, and jury selection is at 9 am. I take the file home, and finish going over that around 9 pm. That is about 13 hours after starting. Like most days, I just fall into bed. I feel like a hamster on a wheel spinning so fast, I can never get off. I just stare, wide-eyed, at the world outside, and pump the wheel as fast as I can, and without any illusion that I am getting anywhere.

✓ *Points to Ponder:*

- What steps would you recommend to Joseph to improve his life?

- What does your practice life have in common with Joseph's?

- What steps can you think of to take, to improve *your* life?

Alicia's Fee Difficulties

Alicia practices real estate, tax and estate litigation in the suburb of a large Eastern city. She writes:

To a certain extent, I have marketed myself as a specialist. The fact is, I feel good about my work — I know I'm good at it. The bottom line is clients always think it is way overpriced, no matter WHAT price. We could be giving it away, they'd complain! I hate hearing that so and so says, 'Oh, she's a great lawyer, she does a good job, but she's SO EXPENSIVE' or hearing from an irate client that they heard from someone at a party that some other attorney does the same work that you did for them but charges only X dollars. Even if the client loves you, he still thinks he overpaid. As lawyers, I think we are angered or hurt by clients telling us they feel 'overcharged.'

Another one I hate is the rich clients who nickel and dime you, who negotiate and complain about every bill, every charge. Who dispute how long you spent on their matter. And the clients who know they have a problem, but who say they can't afford me. I say, 'is this a priority for you?' Sometimes, that's enough, and they somehow come up with the money.

But I hate having to haggle with my clients, constantly arguing with them. It really gets to me.

✓ *Points to Ponder:*

- What steps would you recommend to Alicia to alleviate her fee problem?

- Do you share in Alicia's problem?

- What could you do to alleviate your fee problem?

Randall's Careening Career

Randall is a prominent litigator at a prestigious small firm in a large southwestern city.

Where I am now, doing what I'm doing, came about kind of by default. I was with the firm, doing some of this and some of that, as I started out. The firm just had massive amounts of litigation. I enjoyed the transactional work but they needed more bodies to litigate. After several years, it got to be that was my only real area of expertise. And so in the last couple of years I have been really more thinking about what I want to do, and how I'm going to escape.

Consciously trying to move back away from litigation, but with my history in the firm, litigating just won't let me go. I'll have to break away, to regain any control over the direction of what I do in the law. It's kind of sad. But I have to let go of this place, if I am ever going to live to see 50.

✓ *Points to Ponder:*

- To you, what are Randall's challenges? What steps would you recommend to Randall to meet them?

- What does your career have in common with Randall's?

So there we have three different stories, with a few common threads. I suggest that, as you review their stories again, be looking for the level of control of time each one has, the degree to which their clients have been prepared to understand and both recognize value and benefits, and to pay for them.

How would you restore balance to their lives? To regain balance in your life, you need *control*. Control over your time. Control over your clients. Control over your efforts. To get that control requires that you employ new ways of working with three concepts: *Time, Team,* and *Tools*.

Regaining Balance: Time, Team & Tools

The most common complaint among frustrated lawyers seems to arise from a sense of not having enough time. Yet, we all have exactly the same amount of time: exactly 1,440 minutes in each 24-hour day.

The press of time once had me feeling that way, too. But that is no longer a problem for me. The reason is that I have found how to work with time so productively, that there is always enough time for everything, including large blocks of personal free time. It works because the priorities are set better. Here is how.

Start with Free Time

In order to create the future practice that you want, you must start by determining in advance how much free time you want to have. Paradoxical as it may seem, determining your free time first will actually make it more likely that you will achieve your financial and professional goals, than merely wishing there will be some free time left over afterwards.

I concede this is a radical notion, and difficult to imagine. One lawyer participating in my *Happy Lawyer* teleclasses found himself resisting this idea. He seemed to hear a small voice inside insisting that *"real lawyers don't need time off."* He had fallen into the trap of the grind, the feeling that since there is always work to be done, there is always time for more work.

But the notion that a "real" lawyer must always be doing more, billing more, getting more things done, and feeling guilty when not working, is a lie. It is a trap! As long as you believe that free time, or time off, is what you earn by getting that "one more" phone call in, that "one more" billable hour, that "one more" completed file, then you never get there.

Instead, regard free time as minutes, hours, or days that you "pay yourself first." Free time is the time you keep for yourself. Time to engage in leisure activities with your family, or recreation in the company of friends. The very word, "RE-CREATION," connotes a restorative process, in effect, once again renewing who you are.

Free time is time spent just being who are you, instead of just more and more "doing" what you do for a living. So, begin by determining how many hours a day, days in a week, weeks per quarter, or months per year, over the next few years you want to keep for yourself, for yourself and your family and loved ones.

What do you like to do when you are away from the office? Something that has nothing whatsoever to do with practicing law? Plan some time around those activities.

And it is entirely possible to start small. Just to get the hang of it. One attorney in my teleclasses reported back that the way he successfully got his start to more free time was by making himself a commitment no more radical than merely *to leave the office for home no later than 5:30 pm every night.*

Another found a special way involving her husband. Both of them had been feeling the lack of time together, so they began by scheduling their wedding anniversary as a day to spend together each year, away from their jobs. Next, they scheduled the same date in each of the other eleven months as a similar day together, away from the pressures of careers.

My own solution was to schedule all Fridays as non-office days. The free day was booked on the office calendar as "out of office" like an all-day appointment.

Find the *initial free time action step* that works for you, and take action on it.

Make a Financial Plan

Of course, we cannot spend all our time on leisure, no matter how much enjoyment it might bring us. Instead, we need to continue to achieve our financial requirements and then some. So, determine your financial goals. There are a myriad of books and resources to help you with this. The key for our purposes is that you focus on the amount of time you have determined you will devote to working to achieve your financial goals.

Set down some specifics in terms of budget for personal use, budget for the office, for future growth, for investing in the future, and then figure out what that picture looks like in the future.

Review Your Practice Potential

If you are going to achieve those financial goals in your practice and not rob from your free time, then it is necessary that your practice hours be devoted only to those clients and matters that have the potential to bring you the needed revenues.

So, here are the steps to achieving that:

• determine the time to be devoted to practice

• determine the revenue level needed to meet your financial goals

• review those clients and matters which, if addressed in the allotted time, can produce the desired revenue

Remember, you want to serve the particular people who have the particular need that you get the most satisfaction out of solving. Those clients present you the opportunity to serve them in a way that produces value far above what you can bill on an hourly basis.

But you also must learn to compress delivery of those valued benefits using an organized methodology within your office. That way, you and your people work together to deliver your services and produce the desired revenue in much less time.

That will permit you, over time, to develop a process and a practice that will produce the dollars necessary for you to work only those hours you want and to have as much of the free time off your work as you have planned for, while achieving your financial objectives. I call this *Telescoping.*

Exercise in Telescoping

Summary:
Productivity goals aim at outcomes. Activity goals lay out daily steps to achieve progress.

Steps:

1. *If you knew you could not fail* and you were assured absolutely everything you wanted, in the way of

time, resources, talent, and energy, *what would you choose to do in your profession?*

2. *How much free time* to spend as you choose (family, hobbies, service, recreation, travel) do you want in the next year? Per week? Per month?

3. *How much money* do you want to make as a result of spending your working time on work? Per week? Per month? Per year?

4. What solutions to your *YES! Client's* problems can you provide in a cost effective way?

5. Among the *YES! Clients* you now have and prospects you've identified, *what work can you do that brings them so much value, that benefits them so enormously, that they will pay you the fee income necessary* to earn your goal level?

6. Given how you charge (hourly, project, contingent), how many client engagements will produce the revenues you have envisioned?

✓ *Points to Ponder:*

• Have you clearly identified the steps needed to be accomplished each day you choose to work?

• Do you have the resources you need?

Are you a Lone Ranger? Do you feel that if something is to be done right, you must do it yourself? Lawyers as a rule feel they have all the answers, and that other staff members are there merely to buffer them from the vagaries and interruptions of law practice.

But there is a better way to deliver powerful services to your *YES! Clients.* With your chosen *Arena of Preeminence* in mind, you will want to organize how you run your office with your staff, to maximize their direct and enthusiastic support for your activities in your chosen *Arena of Preeminence.*

Telescoping with a Team

To make the time telescoped into the work days sufficiently productive, you will need to establish your team. You will need to decide what it is that you and only you can deliver to your *YES! Clients*, and then delegate everything else. The process of team-building is not instantaneous. It takes sustained efforts, involving your staff as team members and continually analyzing how better to serve clients.

One starting place is simple communications. Clients have a right to feel that they are regarded as valuable by everyone in your office. Before staff members of your office team can treat clients as genuinely important to the law firm process, your staff must know what it is that makes a client a *YES! Client,* what it is that makes the work you are doing a matter within your *Arena of Preeminence,* and what is in it for them in the goals you are all striving to achieve.

Where the staff has a stake in the process, they will be better able to convey a genuine feeling of appreciation and concern to your clients. The client who feels appreciated and valued is the client that is happy to pay you the premium fees that you are going to be charging. In turn, before your staff can communicate to the clients their central importance, it is necessary for you, the lawyer as leader in your organization, you convey to your staff how crucial they are to the success of the office.

If you have ever participated in team sports, you know how this works. The coach trains people to focus on a mission, such as winning a division or state championship. Even in an individual sport like swimming or wrestling, while each individual makes an individual contribution, it is the team that wins.

Share the Vision of Your *Practice Purpose*

Team members, lawyers, support staff, secretaries, receptionists, file clerks, all need a sense that they are in this effort together. What binds the team is the common *Practice Purpose*: to find, attract, serve and value *YES! Clients* in your *Arena of Preeminence*. That focus not only binds the team together, but also clarifies for your staff how their efforts will best support what you do best.

So, how do we foster teamwork? How do we build sufficient loyalty and common purpose so that members of our firm, from different backgrounds, with different training, experience and qualifications are willing to share the struggle? The key is communication of your vision, your Practice Purpose.

You have developed your vision for your *Arena of Preeminence* to serve your *YES! Clients.* So, bring your staff together and share that vision with them. Together, map out some goals for the organization. Once all the goals are set, all the parties can take part in developing specific plans to implement those goals.

Why? Because all parties have a role to play. The receptionist, the secretarial staff, the paralegals, associate attorneys, anyone who works in your office has a role to play in delivering the result. Therefore, all should be part of developing that plan to implement that service and achieve the goal. Every organization, whether a law firm or any other business, has various functions, all of which must be carried out to be successful. Every law office from one lawyer to a hundred lawyers or more, whether it realizes it or not, also has those functions in its day to day activities. Not all functions should be performed solely by the lawyers. To carry out the goals of the organization consistently, so that team members can both develop professionally and derive job satisfaction, you want specific goals and specific procedures for each team member.

This is a most critical organizational activity. Teamwork becomes possible only to the extent that we involve all members of the firm in developing the plan.

That is why communication is the key. Hearing back from each other among the different roles and functions as to how we are doing on each of these aspects, will also be important to making course corrections, to fine tune the way we are going about things and to make sure the right person is performing the right function.

Let us take a look at what activities you are now doing that should be performed by someone else, freeing you to focus more of your energy on what you do best for your *YES! Clients.*

Here to get you started is an Exercise.

Exercise on Delegation

Summary:
Create team roles to free you to do what only you can do.

Steps:

1. Among all the activities that make up your practice day, what activities and tasks truly require that only you do them?

2. Consider how many activities and tasks could you train someone to do as well as you? List everything that an assistant or other staff member can do.

3. What sort of delegation plan can you devise to free up time to spend on what only you can do?

4. Lay out in a flowchart, grid, list, or however you like, how work might better flow. Take a sample project and map out all the steps.

✓ *Points to Ponder:*

• What is the one project, activity or task which, if delegated to a staff member, would immediately free up for you the greatest amount of time?

• Now, take your list and sit down with your secretary, key assistant, or the entire team, and go over the steps. Ask for suggestions.

• Decide who will take on which steps, in order to free you to focus more of your time on doing those activities you do the best. Modify the plan accordingly. Establish a time period to accomplish the next step in the plan.

These steps will aid you in building a team that is focused both on enabling you to perform at your best and also on your *Practice Purpose* — serving your *YES! Clients* in your *Arena of Preeminence.*

Your team will become more sensitive to the client's perception, and will help you overcome the stereotype of lawyers who are remote, arrogant, and difficult to reach.

Clients who feel their lawyer really cares will result from these steps. That is why networking with your staff is just as important as networking with outside prospects. Your growth as an organization begins with the vision you set yourselves as an organization. Together, you aim for the *YES! Clients* whose major problems you aim to solve through providing your specialized knowledge, skill and devotion to them. Together, you aim to satisfy, even delight and surprise your clients.

Now we will turn to several tools that will aid you in surprising and delighting clients.

Offer a Satisfaction Guarantee

A powerful way to differentiate yourself from other attorneys in your community is to offer a money-back satisfaction guarantee. Of course, you cannot ethically guarantee results, but you can guarantee that the client will be satisfied with your effort and the extent of services that you provide.

In his book *True Professionalism,* professional services firm consultant, David H. Maister, advocates just such a policy. He writes:

Without a guarantee, what is a firm saying to its clients? 'We are committed to your complete satisfaction, but if we fail to please you we expect to be paid anyway!'

But will this work, you ask, in the real world? One attorney's experience reported in the summer of 1997 in *Lawyers Weekly USA* is instructive. A sole practitioner in Ohio reported receiving extraordinary results from this approach. Once his Yellow Page advertisement was changed to read, "no fee if not satisfied" he reports that his practice soared. His policy, if he believes a client's complaint about his services is reasonable, is to refund 100% of the fees. If he thinks the complaint is unreasonable, he will waive the final month of fees. "I don't want to argue about my value," he says. This policy supports the philosophy of creating a trusting relationship with clients. Yet in the first eighteen months, only two clients had requested waivers of fees, and no one had tried to abuse the policy.

A fee guarantee like that motivates you and your entire team to keep professionalism at the forefront in everything that you do, and it can become a powerful part of your *Arena of Preeminence.*

Charging for the Solution, Not by the Hour

I believe that, in the near future, most legal service providers will rapidly move to billing for legal services on the basis of what I call *Solutions Billing.* If you have created an *Arena of Preeminence* and if you are serving your *YES! Client* in every client matter, then you will have positioned yourself and your services to be of extraordinary value.

You are not a commodity. If you effectively juxtapose the real value to the client of the solution against the investment the client must make in order to acquire and own that solution, you can ethically build your fee structure around the solution. Fixed fees for a given engagement or project are enormously well-received by clients.

Do not be in a hurry to set the fee before fully exploring what the clients needs and how you can benefit that client. As you will learn in Chapter Six, you and your client together will explore the issues and set the goals for your engagement. You will have helped them engage their deeper values, and you will have laid out various courses of action and helped your clients select among them.

Explain all the benefits of the chosen solutions, with dollar figures on them, if possible. Quantify the savings, the losses avoided, the rewards gained. And then agree upon and collect your fees based on the perceived value of these solutions.

In my experience, clients respond with pleasure, PLEASURE, at paying fees for perceived value and benefits.

Tracking Your Plan and Your Progress

You will find great value if you will write down your plan, and keep track in a journal or notebook of the steps you are taking, and the results that you get. Then, weekly, monthly, and quarterly, review what has taken place. Chart your progress. Readjust your plan as needed to reflect your experiences.

All right. You have a plan. You know how much telescoped time you will devote to providing value to your *YES! Clients,* and how much time you will save for yourself.

Now, prepare yourself to go out and cultivate the most important group: your *YES! Clients.*

Chapter Five:
Attract the *YES! Clients* You Want

Seek those who find your road agreeable, your personality and mind stimulating, your philosophy acceptable, and your experiences helpful. Let those who do not, seek their own kind.   *-Henri Fabre*

Which are you: a *Lexus* or a *Tercel?* Both automobiles will get you from Point A to Point B. Both are made by the same high-quality manufacturer. But buyers of one gladly pay many times more than buyers of the other.

Given a choice, which would you rather be? Your community's premium-price, top-value attorney in your field? Or just one more fee-sensitive competitor?

If you know there are prospective clients who will gladly pay you premium fees for benefits of high perceived value, is the choice difficult? Of course not. The question is how to attract the clients who are qualified, who will perceive the value, and who are receptive to paying you for it.

Marketing by Differentiation

You have established your *Arena of Preeminence*. Was that not founded upon your own unique ability to solve critical issues and to provide highly valued solutions to your *YES! Clients?* In a similar way, your marketing must differentiate your fundamentally and powerfully original approach to your work and what you provide to clients. Let us look into this a bit more.

Exercise in Differentiating Yourself

Summary:
Differentiation is making you and your practice stand out from the others in a positive light.

Steps:

1. List quickly, with minimum analysis, the characteristics which you feel make you different

from your competitors.

2. Name three or more special qualities in how you serve clients that are not routinely done by other lawyers.

3. Write down those particulars which make you unique in your field.

4. List the qualifications and experiences which enhance that uniqueness in your *Arena of Preeminence.*

✓ *Points to Ponder:*

• Review your answers, and in a sentence, state what you feel are unique aspects to your service.

• State the benefits your clients uniquely receive because they deal with you, as opposed to other lawyers.

- Now, summarize what key changes you would like to make in your practice, to make better use of your uniqueness.

Your Magnetic *Practice Purpose*

What have you found? Can you imagine taking these key ingredients, and presenting them as the magnetic core of your practice? We will turn to several tools and techniques you can use to engage the imaginations of prospects. The power of the vision you create and communicate will draw more and more *YES! Clients*.

You are not looking for mere numbers of clients. You want clients who will be excited to share in your vision, and to benefit from your uniqueness. Those aspects, your vision and your uniqueness, are your magnet. So positioning your practice and marketing your vision will attract your *YES! Clients*. Here are three simple steps:

- Decide that you will devote yourself to being solution oriented

- Clearly identify your *YES! Client*

- Articulate their major concerns or problems and your unique qualification to provide them solutions.

The result will be clients who absolutely *know that they need you*. With the proper phrasing, you can eliminate all doubts. Prospective clients will be attracted so powerfully that they experience an *"Aha!"* moment.

Marketing is the transference of belief. What belief are you trying to convey? That the prospect will benefit more from using you than anyone else, and that you have a passion for providing your chosen clients the optimum solution to what you zero in on as their major problem.

You must be convinced that, because you are ideally suited to provide the solution to that ideal client's major problem, you are uniquely qualified and in that respect completely different from every other lawyer in town.

Why should they believe you? Why should they not think you are in the legal profession for the challenge, as an expression of ego, or in search of influence, affluence, and power? You must convince them that your drive is at a higher level. That your motive is to serve a higher purpose.

No matter whether this purpose initiated your pursuit of a career in the law, or came into view only after years of working in the legal trenches, the motive power of devotion to a deeply held belief or purpose is undeniable.

The loftiest motivation is the career directed and devoted to what the attorney can do in his or her capacity as a lawyer for someone else. Where do you think you are on that scale?

Review your responses to the Exercises from Chapter One. Why are you a lawyer? What caused you to become an attorney? What motivated you then? What motivates you now? If there are indications that a move along this scale would result in greater motivation and satisfaction, how would you describe those indications? What do they tell you?

This emphasis on a higher purpose will set you apart from the crowd of attorneys clamoring for work. You will be positioned as the specialist, providing the needed service and solving their problems. This differentiates you. By stating your positioning convincingly, all questions of the suitability and credibility of your *Practice Purpose* are instantly resolved.

Listeners falling within your group of targeted prospects instantly recognize themselves in your statement and want to know more. Conversely, listeners who are not in your group recognize that sort themselves out. Sound interesting? Here is how to do it.

Exercise on Why I Stand Out

Summary:
You have already delved into many aspects that make you unique. Now, they will make you stand out.

Steps:

1. From your responses to the Exercises in Chapters One and Two, make a list of all the ways you developed in which a client will be better off to choose you instead of some other lawyer in your community.

2. Now develop a statement of benefits that succinctly says how that is the case.

3. Next, trim the key benefits you deliver into one provocative statement.

4. List three to five key differences that distinguish your approach from most lawyers in your field of law.

Now you have listed a number of factors that you believe make what you offer both distinctive and more valuable. Next, you must consistently and powerfully communicate this belief to people. One of the very best ways to do this is with a "spoken logo." Let me explain.

Create a "Spoken Logo"

Why is it that commercial advertising campaigns use slogans? Why has electoral politics boiled down to sound bites? I think it is because of the pace at which we live our lives. Our ever shorter attention spans. The clamor for our attraction for just long enough to make a quick judgment of, "yes, that's me," or "no, that's not me."

Whether the choice is a brand of beer, or an approach to domestic policy, we are bombarded with brief, insistent messages. The purpose of these messages is to attract and repel. Attract the targeted audience, and repel the rest. Pull in the interested consumer or voter, and forget about the rest.

How have you done in your practice? Without intending it, have you been attracting all the wrong clients? When you have been asked, "So, what do you do for a living?" have you ever merely replied, "I am an attorney"? What a wasted opportunity!

Wouldn't you prefer to respond with a brief, attention-getting message that excites interest? A message that quickly empowers your prospective *YES! Client* with the means for immediate self-recognition? That is what a properly thought-out spoken logo will do for you.

Your spoken logo is a succinct and provocative high-impact presentation of your personal *Practice Purpose*. It is stated in terms of benefits. Think of it as your 30-second or 15-second commercial.

Your spoken logo excites curiosity. A good spoken logo prompts further inquiry by your listeners. Here are two famous examples.

> **"Fresh pizza delivered hot within 30 minutes or it's free."**

> **"When it absolutely, positively has to be there overnight."**

What gives these statements their power? No first-person reference is made to the advertiser. Instead, each statement focuses on benefits. The message is all about the reward received by those using the service — "a fast, hot pizza," or "guaranteed next day package delivery."

Moreover, each spoken logo screens out those whom the company does not want to attract. People who hate pizza, or who have no urgent package delivery needs, are not likely to be pulled by these statements. Let us take a closer look at the actual elements.

Elements of a *Spoken Logo*

- *Each statement is succinct.* Ten words or less.

- *Each statement is "catchy."* In the pop music business, each song has a "hook." The hook attracts and retains the listener's attention with some distinctive phrase or rhythm ("absolutely, positively"). That element of sound or sense remains memorable.

- *Each statement makes one main promise.* The statement leads with the benefit, and then makes a provocative promise ("within 30 minutes").

- *Each statement ends with a close.* The close is that part that is the end result or guarantee, as in "or it's free" and "when it has to be there overnight".

Now take these elements and build your own spoken logo. Your spoken logo must open with a result, benefit, outcome or reward that is relevant to the listener you want to attract. Avoid saying, "I'm an attorney." Say something that flags the problem solved or loss avoided.

Tightly match your statement closely to the people you want to attract. The closer the fit, the more effective your spoken logo. Moreover, you want your spoken logo to attract only listeners who can benefit from your service and repel all the others, whom you do not want to attract. Let me illustrate with a helpful technique for delivering your spoken logo.

My Spoken Logo

As an estate planning attorney, I see all too often unplanned or inadequately planned family situations. Because of lack of planning, there may be exposure to unnecessary taxes, or even forced liquidation or sale of a business or properties in order to pay estate taxes.

So, among my most eligible prospects are business owners and real estate investors. I use a spoken logo like this. I am asked: *"What do you do?"*

"I provide people peace of mind and maximum tax savings." (Prominent Promise)

"Really? How?"

"Well, you know how families of business owners or real estate investors sometimes end up selling off the business or property, just to pay taxes? Like when Joe Robbie's family had to sell the Miami Dolphins football team to pay the government?"

"Yeah?"

"Well, I help folks arrange things for peace of mind now, and to keep Uncle Sam out of their pocket later."

The listeners' next reaction usually either qualifies them as prospective clients or rules them out. Business owners and real estate investors usually ask me, *"How do you do that?"* I go on to explain how we approach estate planning.

Others often remark that they have no estate to speak of, not having a business or real estate. So I will follow up with a question about life insurance, because I find that most people do not know that life insurance increases the size of the taxable estate. I mention that many people with insurance may benefit from planning by reason of that alone. That may be enough to qualify them as prospects.

Either way, I have focused on the market I want — clients with sizeable holdings. My spoken logo makes a

Prominent Promise. And my listeners respond and rule themselves in or out.

My spoken logo accomplishes the following seven things:

Function or Result	Phrase
Make Prominent Promise	"Peace of mind, Maximum Tax Savings"
Draw curiosity	"You know how . . .?"
Portray *YES! Clients*	"families, business owners, investors"
Show loss or pain	"forced to sell assets to pay taxes?"
Make it real	"Miami Dolphins owners"
Be solutions provider	"what I do is help arrange things now"

| Benefits, benefits | "Peace of mind now, and lower taxes later." |

Remember, your listener does NOT care about what you do. Your listener only cares about what the listener might get out of what you do! You must tap into the listener's emotions in some way, paint an appealing or intriguing picture, and tantalize the listener to want to know more.

Now it is your turn. Here is an Exercise to help you create your own spoken logo.

Exercise for Creating Your *Spoken Logo*

Summary:
Put elements of a spoken logo together for your practice.

Steps:

Write down the following as each applies to your practice.

1. Your *Prominent Promise:*

2. How you make it real: ("You know how. . .?"

3. Short, powerful benefits description" ("What I do is...")

✓ *Points to Ponder:*

- Is it succinct?

- Does it make one main promise?

- Is it "catchy?"

- Will your prospective *YES! Client* have an "Aha!" moment of self-recognition?

Marketing Your Way to Preeminence

Now, you want to make that spoken logo the heart of all your marketing efforts, to promote your practice and yourself.

Your practice is the solution to that major problem. Once you have sufficiently targeted the *YES! Clients*, you can replicate the message continually, only if you market it.

What do you already enjoy doing? Writing? Speaking? Socializing? Any of these activities can your pathway to preeminence.

Select from among them the best marketing tools for you and your practice. Pick what appeals to you. Then tailor the activity to project your message.

Remember the key concept: individual Americans have no way of judging the value of one legal service provider versus another. They simply do not know. As a result, you, the professional, must help the client identify their expectations and then offer to fulfill them.

Stress Benefits, Not Features

Be forthright about the benefits that the client will receive by working with you. Your emphasis should be turned around so that the client, the prospect, the reader, sees and hears tangible benefits to be received through your services. In all your written materials, you want to abolish "features," and instead stress "benefits."

What is a feature? It is about you, your firm, your activities. For example:

"At Blowhard and Wheedle, we provide legal services in all areas of domestic relations, personal injury, and criminal defense. Our 'state of the art' legal library includes the very latest in Internet resources for comprehensive research support, and our staff are trained to assist our litigators in their trial work."

What is a benefit? It is about your client and his or her needs, and about how you will meet those needs.

"Before it costs you a dime, you will know exactly what you can expect in working on your landlord-tenant matter. You will receive a no-cost, no-obligation consultation, to share the nature of your problem and receive answers to your questions. You will learn exactly

The Happy Lawyer

how your legal fees will be set, and what the process will entail."

See the difference? Review *your* written materials, such as your firm brochure, and any other materials. Do they merely extol your credentials and features of your service? Or do they stress benefits to clients? Scrap any materials that do not fit this rule and start over.

Another marketing tool that you can offer is a list of resources. Where can your *YES! Client,* who has a particular kind of need, obtain the information or service that would help them understand more about how to solve their problem?

Furnish Information

You as a practitioner can make available resource information, both to prospective clients, and to related professionals. Articles that you author or that you get permission to reproduce are especially powerful marketing tools. Teaching other professionals about your specialty helps build your referral network of

126

professionals. These allied fields may have the kinds of clients that you would like to work with. You have determined that you possess unique strengths and abilities.

In your *Arena of Preeminence,* you are the expert. Expand your image with information provided to clients and prospects that enhance your identification as an expert in your particular field.

Attorneys write all the time. Yet many feel writing an article is too daunting a challenge. The key is to have a systematic way to produce a useable piece.

Here is a step-by-step method to get an article down on paper quickly. Think you can't produce a brief readable article that will appeal to your prospects? Try it and see.

Exercise in Writing an Article the Easy Way

Summary:
Provides an easy format to produce non-technical articles.

Steps:

1. Pick your topic.

2. Quickly jot down or dictate as many key words or concepts, with NO detail or elaboration, as you can in 30 seconds.

3. Now group the phrases or key words into 3 key points you would like to make.

4. Under each of the 3 key points, jot down or dictate a sentence or two for each of the phrases or key words.

5. Cut and paste the text until it flows logically and smoothly.

6. Add a three-sentence introductory paragraph, that states the problem or topic, suggests the answer, and states that you will explain.

7. Add a brief conclusion that mirrors the introductory paragraph, restating the problem or topic; summarizing the answers, and state the actions you suggest will benefit the reader.

8. Always add a "tag" to your article with contact information. This way, your readers will know how to reach you.

✓ *Points to Ponder:*

• Why not stress your *Arena of Preeminence* with a series of articles based on the ten questions you are most frequently asked?

• How about a "special report" for your best referral sources answering their need to know about your field and how they can serve their clients better with this information?

How to Make Use of Your Article

Local papers are always in need of information. An article on your specific field may just fill that need. Call your local newspaper and ask to speak to a features editor. Once you have a name, offer to send that specific editor the article. Such articles are often printed virtually as submitted.

You can submit a more formal article related to your *Arena of Preeminence* to your local bar association or a wider law publication. Be sure to get their editorial guidelines ahead of time, so you can present your article in the publication's preferred format.

If it is published, be sure to obtain reprints. Send a copy to every allied professional you know or would like to know.

Or, you can choose not to seek publication, and instead create enhanced value by simply printing the article on your own letterhead as a "Special Report," for clients and referral sources.

If you do not want to take the time to write your own, you can enhance your own professional stature with works by others, like books and articles. Find materials with a point of view with which you agree. You will need to obtain permissions or to buy reprints, but there is a host of material available if you will put your imagination to work on it.

Buy a stamp that says "courtesy of . ." or "for your information" and reproduces your name, your address and a date. Use it to stamp every single item that you give or send out.

Trade publishers like *Dearborn Financial* and *Wiley & Sons* publish a wide variety of high quality paperback titles. Many are focused on the very benefits your clients want: how to make more money, save money, avoid loss, plan for retirement, buy property, and many other timely topics. It is easy to establish a quantity purchase, wholesale account with such publishers. Then you can either sell or give away titles appropriate to those in your *Arena of Preeminence.*

Smart Marketing with Seminars

Many lawyers put on seminars. But most seminars by attorneys emphasize turgid technical material. They violate the rule that you should "stress benefits, not features." While you are feeding your audience's hunger for information, you must also articulate the benefits that come from working with you. So build your seminar on providing information that speaks to fears and concerns first, with technical "how-to"s later. Some other suggestions:

✓ *Always offer a "take home" piece.* This may be a brochure, a summary of points covered, or a copy of a published article.

✓ *Always give out a sheet and ask for comments.* You learn about your presentation, your materials, the information and any other items of interest to your audience.

✓ *Always provide an incentive for them to contact you.* This may be a special offer of a free consultation, or further opportunity to go into depth as to their particular interest or need.

✓ *Always give credit to your sponsor.* In my experience, self-sponsored seminars have about one-third the attendance of an event with a third-party sponsor. So, I like to speak at events hosted by some related professional.

Supercharging Your Social Network

Your practice will expand faster based on relationships than anything else. The increase in networking and "leads" clubs whose members congregate to trade leads for each other's businesses offers you an opportunity for social interaction where you can let people know what you do, and whom it can benefit. Repeated contacts with these individuals and organizations will build relationships.

Be sensitive to the group's perspective. Offer to provide information or assistance if it is appropriate. Offer your assistance, information, training, or continuing education classes. Find a way to make that professional organization a part of your team to help you deliver even better service to your clients.

You are a specialist with a *Practice Purpose*. Through your network, marketing and educational efforts, you offer valuable information to other professionals and to their prospective clients. This fosters your image as a professional who is client-oriented and knowledgeable.

Making Alliances That Work

Join forces with others who already have as customers or clients those people or companies that you would like to have. You already know there are such companies and professionals with such clients and customers.

You can enjoy many referrals from the other professionals to come and work together with you to solve their clients' problems. The key here is to forge alliances with other professionals *who are not in competition with you.* They provide services that do not compete with yours, but *their customers or clients have the same characteristics as your YES! Clients.* Together you can team up and present greater value to these clients.

In order to succeed in making fruitful alliances, you must have a ready answer to the nagging question that will inevitably occur in your prospective alliance partner's mind: *What's in it for me?*

You must develop several compelling reasons that show that, by teaming up together, their customer or client will gain benefits not otherwise available. Here is an Exercise to help develop those reasons.

Exercise on Your Potential Allies

Summary:
Systematically identify potential sources of allies whose clients you can benefit.

Steps:

1. List 10 non-competitor contacts whose clients fit your *YES! Clients.*

2. Describe the benefits you could provide to these clients.

3. Describe the information your contacts need to have handy to remind them of your benefits to their clients or customers. A "special report," a "resources guide," reprints of articles, a book or audiotape? Brainstorm. Come up with at least three.

4. Jot down several phrases describing the benefits for their clients.

5. Write a letter to your contacts, presenting these ideas and potential benefits to them and their clients. Ask to meet with them to discuss and get their reactions and suggestions. Send out and follow up with phone or personal contacts.

With these techniques, you will find your contacts opening up to you, sensing your concern for them and their relationships with their clients. Then, you can tailor your presentation and your materials to what will help them help their customers, and in turn, that will help you gain access to a new source of *YES! Clients.*

Finally, you can multiply your opportunity to work with *YES! Clients* through building referrals as a steady source of new business.

How to Enjoy More (and Better!) Referrals

Why are referrals the single most important tool to expand your dominance in your *Arena of Preeminence?* Because referrals from your *YES! Clients* will put you in touch with others who are like them. They will refer to others with the same needs and characteristics, who are facing the same challenges and problems your practice is designed to solve.

Have you ever wondered why you do not receive more referrals? The answer lies in a simple fact: *An astounding 70% of clients surveyed are unaware that their attorney, with whom they were fully satisfied, welcomed referrals!* The rest either did not believe that their lawyer was accepting new business, or did not know one way or the other.

So how do you go about making referrals happen? First, stop waiting for them! You have to take a simple first step — **ASK**. The more you ask, the more referrals you get.

How you ask will make all the difference. Why? Because your satisfied clients right now do not even know that you want referrals. Once you talk to them in the right way, they will happily refer business to you.

Are you afraid that asking somehow suggests that you are not successful? Or will create doubt or fear in clients that they might regret having made a referral because they fear you may pester their friends? Want to overcome your fear of asking for referrals?

Here's how. Focus again on your purpose in providing your *YES! Clients* with the solutions to their most significant problems. Let your clients know early on in the engagement that you hope that they will be prepared to refer once your services have satisfied them. Tell them your *Practice Purpose*, and you wish to bring others the same benefits they are receiving. Create that expectation.

A referral from your satisfied client, properly handled, is like a powerful endorsement of you to your new prospect. Not only does the prospect receive your name from someone they already know and regard favorably, but also the prospect begins a relationship with you with an expectation of both excellence and value.

Action Steps to More Referrals

Drawn from David M. Ward's excellent work *Referral Magic, The Complete Guide to Attracting New Clients and Developing a Successful Law Practice!* here are some action steps to improve your referrals.

1. Reinforce client's satisfaction. Ask, "Tell me, Mr. Client, have you been satisfied with the work we've done for you?"

2. Ask for your client's help. Explain the importance to expanding your practice of receiving qualified referrals from satisfied clients, and ask that they assist you.

3. Stress benefits. Explain how their referrals to you will benefit them. If seeking referrals within a particular group or industry, suggest how your *Arena of Preeminence* benefits them by your superior specialized expertise, helping them ward off problems, save money and avoid unpleasant surprises.

4. Teach them what you are looking for. Teach them to recognize your prospective *YES! Clients*. Clients often fail to refer simply because you have not taught them enough about the services you provide, the problems you solve, the benefits you provide and the clients you serve and want to serve more of.

5. *Provide reassurance.* Reassure them that referring will not embarrass them, that you will not reveal any confidential information about them or their matters to any person whom they may refer. Remind them of your ethical obligation and professional commitment to confidentiality.

6. *Use specifics to help bring faces to mind.* Make it easy to gather referrals, with a professional and polished presentation of your request. A form will both assure that you do not overlook anything, and show the importance that you place on referrals in your practice. To help them bring to mind prospective referrals, ask in context, like employment, business or trade groups, and clubs they belong to. When you ask: "Who do you know who . . . ?" fill in the first blank with the context. *E.g.*, "Who do you know in the Widget Manufacturers Association. . .?" The use of "who" assumes that the client does in fact know someone. The context calls to mind specific faces and names as soon as you fill in the blank. Finish the question with the specific characteristics of your *YES! Client.*

7. *Explain the steps.* Tell them exactly how to make a referral. If you want to mail a letter or report to a referral, explain that. If you prefer that the referral call you, give your client the phone number, explain what or whom the referral should ask for when they call, what to do if you're not in. Make it as easy as possible. The easier it is, the more likely your clients will refer.

8. *Remember to ask.* Ask for referrals often. The more often you ask, the more often you receive. Ask at the peak point of satisfaction with your services, usually toward the conclusion of your engagement, when you have delivered all of the key benefits and your client's appreciation is high.

Never be embarrassed to ask for referrals. Referrals benefit everyone — your client, your clients' referrals to you, and you yourself.

Remember, too, to say "thank you." Send a thank you for each referral, even those who do not become a client. Show how much you appreciate referrals with a handwritten, short, personalized note. *Referral Magic* contains an excellent section on writing very effective short, personalized thank-you notes.

Make an organized referral effort an indispensable part of your practice. You will see an appreciable increase in the duration of your client relationships, as well as an increase in the right kind of clients seeking your services.

Becoming a Master Marketer

Marketing is the communication of conviction and belief. In this Chapter, we have discussed powerful techniques to bring you clients. Differentiation and standing out in a positive light. Making known your *Practice Purpose.* Creating a *Spoken Logo.* Creating marketing materials. Speaking and networking. Forging synergistic alliances. Building with referrals.

Whichever combination of these techniques you use, your credibility above all will make your marketing efforts effective. You will find yourself most believable when dealing with people whom you know, and who already know you. Therefore, the most effective marketing takes place within the context of relationships.

Relationships of Trust

Relationships with your clients, referrals and alliance partners will provide the setting for your proclamation of your *Practice Purpose,* and bring dominance of your *Arena of Preeminence.*

The qualified prospects and referrals will come in ever increasing numbers. Next, you need to hone your skills in one-on-one dealings with them, through powerful communications.

Your Notes

Chapter Six:
Building Trust Through Breakthrough Communications

If you want to be listened to, you should put in time listening.
— *Marge Piercy*

Clients who feel that they have been heard will both trust you more and value you more. This leads to two enormous benefits. First, the client who feels heard will form a better bond with you, inherently more satisfying to both lawyer and client. Second, the client who feels heard will be more open and receptive to your portrayal of the benefits you offer and to the value of your services. That opens the door to higher fees, more cheerfully paid.

You will gain greater fulfillment dealing with clients if you will improve your listening skills. The tools of communication will serve you well. Even more powerful is the effect of listening on your ability to be paid what you are worth.

In this Chapter, we will explore how to improve your skills and apply them, so as to reap the rewards of personal and financial satisfaction.

What are the elements of this approach? They are:

- Differentiation of you from other lawyers by stressing your communications, your new way of working with clients

- Client communications and conferences that put clients in charge and build trust

- Active listening and reflecting to clients

- Exploring and finding agreement on the situation, the problem, the goals

- Enabling your clients to choose the solution that best meets their needs

Working with clients is really the key to this entire approach. Until your clients really know the value of what your solution will do for them, your services are absolutely worthless.

It is like the old saying that "people do not care how much you know, until they know how much you care." But you can stand out from all the other lawyers in your community, and can turn the stereotype of the arrogant attorney on its head. Because you will not talk down to your clients. You will not impose dogmatic opinions on them.

Instead, you will engage in a mutual teaching and learning process. You will ask questions, and listen to the answers. You will use some special techniques that will raise the client's confidence in your regard for the client's concerns.

This process will connect you to your client. Then you can actually address the problems that you can solve. And you will learn what outcome will best appeal to and fulfill their underlying values and emotion. I call this approach *Finding the Success Solution*.

Finding the *Success Solution*

The *Success Solution* when uncovered together will excite your clients. They will respond both in terms of the actual issue or problem, and also in terms of their subjective perception of how it fits them, their values, their beliefs, and their emotions.

You must learn what the *Success Solution* looks like to your client. How do you uncover this? As the listener, you must learn to receive, and then feed back and restate and confirm what has been heard. It takes . . .

> *Listening* ⟶ *Reflection* ⟶ *Trust* ⟶
> *Agreement* ⟶ *Collaboration* ⟶ *Success Solution*

All communication with your clients occurs at both a nonverbal and a verbal level. You listen with a special kind of attention, to receive the kind of information that is helping you to understand what matters most to this particular client. And you employ simple but powerful techniques to create a higher level of trust with your clients than you have ever experienced.

Six Steps to Higher Trust Level with New Clients

1. *Put them at ease at the initial conference.*

One way to do this is to make sure they understand what if anything they will be charged. Make sure they understand what this initial charge covers, or if the conference is free, so that they will not look at their watch and worry about time charges. You want them to feel that they can take the time to open up to you.

2. *Ask right away,* ***How can I help you?***

Find out what it is that is foremost on their mind. This will give you an opening to get to higher values or deeper motivations and needs that will become part of your relationship with them.

3. *Eliminate artificial barriers.*

Meet them at a round table or a desk with nothing on it but their own file folder and your notepad. Show them that your focus is entirely upon them. No phone calls, no interruptions, just them and you and their issues.

4. *Seek Deeper Values to Serve.*

Become devoted to serving your clients' better natures, helping them achieve their loftiest goals and fulfill their deepest values. Adapt and master the *Values Conversation* approach pioneered by Bill Bachrach, discussed below.

5. *Listen twice as much as you speak.*

Spend twice as much of your time **listening** as you do **speaking**. Separate the writing down of notes from maintaining steady eye contact.

As you are listening to them, look them in the eye. Then, when you restate what they say, and receive their agreement, that is the time when you can look down to make your notes. Read them back step-by step and ask the client for their affirmation that you are getting it down right. This affirmation will help you, it will clarify things, and it helps the client feel that you truly care.

6. *Summarize and ask permission to proceed.*

Suggest ways to go forward based on a summarized set of information, goals and priorities. Offer alternative courses of action. Explore the degree of the client's readiness to take action. Obtain a commitment to act or to revisit in the next 48 hours or so.

Finding the client's *Success Solution* through this method of communication makes time a friend both to you and to your client.

You are working on building trust, in order that you can collaborate together to uncover the keys to your client's *Success Solution*. Clients will pay mightily for the solution to what is bothering them.

Clients pay happily when they see value of what you are doing for them. You have spelled out in advance how the process will work, making time your client's friend, too.

Your Client As Partner in the *Success Solution*

Your goal here, once trust is firmly established, is to involve your client deeply in the process of finding the solution. So, in a sense, your client becomes a partner in the process. Your job is to educate, then collaborate and get agreement.

When agreement is achieved, the result will be a high perceived value, which translates to higher fees. This cannot be done by the clock. This means that your process of engagement and discussion at your first and subsequent meetings helps to define the client's idea of a successful outcome. The client's understanding of what goals, if achieved, constitute success.

To engage in better listening means more than mere fact gathering. Better listening is the heart of a more powerful client connection. Poor listening is a major component of lawyers' failure to bond with clients.

It is no wonder that a leading expert and trainer in the field of business communications has written that ineffective listeners are viewed as boorish, self-centered, disinterested, preoccupied and socially unacceptable.

Notice a resemblance to any lawyer stereotype? We are simply not taught to listen. Five factors contribute to our failure to listen effectively. How many fit you?

- *Listening is hard work.* You must concentrate on the other person. It is just plain hard, so many of us do not do it.

- *"Shields are up."* Our habitual screening out of excess stimuli often leads us to screen out important things as well.

- *Hurried thinking.* We rush to get ahead of the other person. We think we know what they are going to say, so we interrupt, not waiting to hear them out.

- *Speed gap.* There is gap in speed between the speed of thought and the speed of speech. Speech, at 135 to 175 words a minute is outstripped by listening, which can go 400 to 500 words a minute easily. Poor listeners spend that time daydreaming, jumping to conclusions, planning their reply or mentally arguing with what is being said.

* *Lack of training.* Most of us simply have no training in listening. Hearing does not equate to listening. This means that there is only something like a 25% effectiveness rate, meaning 75% of what we hear is lost or misunderstood.

Where are you on that list? Do you recognize yourself, perhaps in the crush of time mentally getting on to the next task or thinking about keeping the next appointment? If so, you are really not present. You are not "there" for those clients, and they sense your distraction. Your seeming preoccupation leaves them with a feeling of emotional distance, and they resent it. Want to overcome that distance? Use *Active Listening.*

Start Using Active Listening

What most lawyers do is "fact gathering." This communications style is above all utilitarian. That is, it seeks and deals with information only if it has objective factual value. It certainly has an indispensable role to play in working with clients. But by its very nature, fact gathering is of neutral or negative value to the forging of a bond between client and attorney. Fact gathering will not create trust.

Active listening on the other hand, means listening for the emotional content beneath what a speaker is saying, and doing something with that content. The "active listener" listens, then evaluates and reflects that emotional content to the speaker. That assists the speaker to feel more comfortable and more fully understood. It creates a nonverbal connection that leads to trust.

Active listening is hard work. There are three parts:

- *Active waiting.* Focusing on the other person's message, not your reply.

- *Empathizing.* Quickly calling to mind analogous experiences you have had.

- *Finding the Words.* "Reflecting" by restating the essence of the other person's message, with an emphasis on their feelings.

The active listener is involved with the speaker's nonverbal emotional communication. This emphasis on feelings is critically important. The feedback that the active listener gives the speaker conveys to the speaker whether the communication has in fact been successful.

An active listener gets affirmation, correction or more information in response to their feedback. The speaker thus feels emotional satisfaction from having been heard. A closer relationship results. In our situation that leads to greater trust than we might otherwise have.

The Power of Reflecting

One simple yet powerful technique to let people know we have heard them, is called *reflecting*. Reflecting conveys your understanding and reduces any misunderstanding.

Reflecting means restating what you have heard and then letting the other person either affirm, amplify or correct it. In doing so, you are learning what is on your client's mind. You will miss the opportunity, though, to deepen your relationship and increase your value to your client unless you reflect the emotional content back to the client.

For example, in a conference with a client on an injury case, the client may allude to fears of testifying at trial. You have several choices: you can ignore those fears, and brush them off — (*"I'll prepare you beforehand, nothing to worry about"*). You can put them down — (*"That's really nothing to worry about"*). Or you can forge a powerful connection with your client by reflecting their fear — (*"You sound worried about having to testify"*).

When the client responds affirmatively, you can explore what is behind that feeling. Are they afraid of being caught in a falsehood? Or being embarrassed? With each reflection, ask for affirmation of the importance that they have put on it. This gives the client an opportunity to clarify their feelings to you.

When you have engaged in this type of exchange a number of times, they will feel heard. And probably you will have developed a strategy together to deal with the problem more effectively than had the issue not been brought, through your reflecting, to the surface.

Beginning to use these techniques is awkward. So, preparing a script for yourself will aid you to get started.

Exercise to Prepare an Active Listening Script

Summary:
Prepare handy phrases for active listening in next conference.

Steps:

1. To prepare a script for an upcoming initial client meeting, jot down some notes of areas or events common to such a situation.

2. Then create several versions of reflective statements, along the following pattern:

You felt _____ and _____ when _____.

Examples: *"You felt puzzled and uncertain when his response to your request for a divorce was silence."*

   "The loss of your husband has left you confused and fearful, especially with regard to finances."

   "Your former partner's claim came as a surprise and you felt hurt and angry."

Your script:

When _____, you felt _____ and _____.

You felt _____ and _____ when _____.

3. At the client meeting, try out your listening skills. In addition to getting content and facts, listen for and reflect back the underlying emotional content.

✓ *Points to Ponder:*

*   How does your client react to your scripted response?

*   Does your client supply you more information, perhaps with a heightened brightness and enthusiasm or emphasis?

Combine Reflecting with Questioning

Reflective statements restate in your words the contents of what the client has just said, highlighting the emotional aspect (*"you felt ..."*). Questioning in turn will elicit specifics that you can pin down (*"Now, was this before or after. . . ?"*)

Be sure you provide somewhere for the conversation to go, all the time reassuring the client that their concerns have been heard.

Avoid making any judgment on feelings expressed. This is critical, so just acknowledge the emotional content in a completely non-judgmental way. This is hard sometimes to do.

Even a seemingly innocent statement in response to strong emotion (*"I certainly don't blame you for feeling that way"*) conveys a judgment. It is as deadening to the empathetic connection to say that as it is to respond to strong emotions with a statement like, *"Oh, I wouldn't go as far as that!"*

Avoid making any statement that implies a judgment critical of their expressed emotion. The reaction will be either to argue with you, in a tone of hurt self-justification, or to subconsciously decide you are not emotionally trustworthy and simply stop revealing themselves to you.

But through your skilled role of providing non-judgmental acceptance, you will build empathy, which leads to trust.

Seek Agreement

You want to reach agreement on the meaning of the situation, the problem that they face and its implications. You learn this through the interplay, attending to both facts and feelings. You ask what is important about each issue, then you reflect the feelings back to the clients.

Now you must seek agreement on the meaning of it all. Your goal is to reconfirm both the explicit and implicit in what your client has been telling you. This you must do before you can thoroughly review and restate each and every client goal and objective that arise out of the situation. These are the foundation questions for your relationship and the heart of the value your clients will perceive in the solutions that you offer. After all, value is going to come from the solutions you offer to the problems that they have presented.

You cannot really set a value on your services until your clients and you have fully explored their situation and determined what is really important about the solutions that you can offer to them. You want to empower the client to chose the optimal solutions to meet their needs.

At each step along the way, clients are handing you the information you need to help them, yet superficial listening will yield only superficial understanding, leading to a solution that addresses things on the surface but lacks the power to deeply satisfy your client at the level of their values. Such an approach will not reach them deeply. To truly satisfy your client you need to uncover their values that surround whatever the problem is.

Finding Clients' Deeply Held Personal Values

Why are values so critical to explore with new or prospective clients? Values are the key to whether or not there is a future to an attorney-client relationship with this person. Second, a client's deeply held values are the most significant motivators you can reach and appeal to, as you offer your *Practice Purpose* and the resulting benefits to a prospective *YES! Client.* Values form the basis of a deep and lasting relationship built on trust and mutual respect. *In order to achieve the highest benefits, you must work with the highest values that a client holds dear.*

So how do you do this in a useful, yet tactful way? After all, most of us could not really articulate our values in isolation. They exist in a bundle that is complex and often contradictory. We are often insecure about them and questioning that is too direct makes us defensive, embarrassed, fearful and resentful, especially by a stranger. Clients that you question may even fudge things in rather blatant ways just to relieve the psychological discomfort that arises from too direct a questioning style.

Values are not why the client came to you, but they are motivators that will either lead to clients entering into your process and receiving the benefits you offer, or they will not. Values are where trust is built. Delving into the arena of values will communicate early on that you care about the client, not merely about the client's money and ability to pay your fees. Finally, starting with values will greatly enhance the value the client will place on your services, and it will be reflected in the fees they pay you.

Lead into a Values Conversation and Then Listen

But if listening is so important at the first meeting, then how do you establish your authority? If you are mostly asking questions and listening, how do you know whether you have someone with whom you can work? Good questions. The leading authority on how advisors can respect and build upon the importance of values in building relationships of trust with clients, calls the approach engaging in a *Values Conversation*.

Bill Bachrach's excellent book entitled, *Values-Based Selling: The Art of High-Trust Client Relationships for Financial Advisors, Insurance Agents and Investment Reps*, goes into detail. I will just hit the high points here, and then give one example of how you might adapt this method to your law practice.

Ride the Elevator to the Top with "WIA*TY?"

If clients store their values away from prying eyes, you need a quick way to arrive at their "top floor." The fastest "elevator" is the *Values Conversation*. Each floor is reached by means of what Bachrach calls the "WIA*TY" question. In his field of training financial professionals, the asterisk specifically stands for the word "money" because it underlies everything that they deal in. So their fundamental WIA*TY question is *"What's important about money to you?"* The advisor sets the stage is with a brief, logical explanation of why she is asking. The advisor might say, *"Your taking the time to meet with me today tells me that you must be serious about making smart choices with your money. Is that true?"* When the client replies, *"Yes, I am,"* the advisor then asks, with genuine interest, *"Help me understand. What's important about money to you?"* Then **she listens to the answer.** This is a values *conversation,* not an interrogation. Here's an example.

Perhaps the client says, *"I would like to have enough money to have more free time."* The advisor writes down the key word in the client's response ("free time"). The advisor has now entered the elevator on the first floor, but with a goal, not a value. Free time is a goal — it is about "achieving" or "having." Values fulfill and satisfy. They are about "being."

In order to press the elevator button and go up to the second floor, the advisor resets the stage, and asks the next question. *"That's interesting. What's important about free time to you?"* The client says, *"I have some projects I want to work on."*

We're now on the second floor. The advisor resets the stage and again asks the WIA*TY question. *"Projects mean a lot of different things to different people, so just so I get a clear picture here, what's important about the projects you want to work on to you?"* The client replies with a description of involvement in volunteer work.

Third floor. The advisor resets the stage, and asks, *"WIA that volunteer work TY?"* A few more repetitions, resetting the stage, and asking the WIA*TY question follow, and then the client describes the wonderful sense of making a difference in other people's lives that she feels growing out of her involvement with this particular organization.

Testing with the Confirming Question

The advisor has uncovered a core value, and to find out whether she has reached the top of the client's elevator, she asks the *Confirming Question.* That question is, *"Is there anything more important to you than [the last value mentioned]?"* In our example, the question would be *"Is there anything more important to you than that sense of making a difference in other people's lives?"*

If the answer is yes, then there are still more flights to go up. The advisor resets the stage and asks the reformulated WIA*TY question again, and continues until she feels again that the top of the elevator has been reached, and tests it with the Confirming Question.

Get a Pre-Commitment to a Working Relationship

When the answer to the Confirming Question is no, there is nothing more important than *[the last stated value],* then it is time is seek the client's pre-commitment to a working relationship. Use the Pre-commitment Question: *"Suppose we could create a strategy that would help you make the smart financial choices,* the choices that would let you have the **time freedom** you want, so you could **work on the projects you find important** and valuable, and spend **more time on the charity work** you love so much, and would allow you to enjoy that **wonderful sense of making a real difference in people's lives.** If that were the case, would you and I have a basis for working together?"

Note the Pre-commitment question is built with goals and values from each floor of the elevator ride to the top. It shows clients how important their goals and values are to the advisor. An affirmative answer, and the advisor and client have established a basis for a working relationship of trust, directed at helping to achieve the client's goals and fulfill her values.

Transitioning Off the Elevator

The Pre-commitment allows a transition into better fact-finding with a client who now understands that full disclosure will assist the advisor to help them reach their goals and serve their values. Finally, it leads to a professional engagement that includes understanding how the advisor works and agreement on how the client pays.

Starting with the *Values Conversation* lets you lead by listening. Let us see how you can use this in your practice. Not only will you better understand your client's problem so that you can offer better solutions, but you will gain influence and credibility with your client. Let me give you an example.

Suppose you are meeting with a young couple who have a new baby, and who have come in because they have been told they should name a guardian in a Will. You might set the stage with, *"Your making time to see me when you have the hectic life of new parents tells me you are serious about making arrangements to care for [baby's name] if anything should happen to you. Am I right?"* They answer *"Yes, we are."*

You reset the stage and ask the WIA*TY question. *"Okay, for me to help you select the right person to be guardian of [baby's name] if anything happened to you, help me* *understand, what's important about who the guardian of your child is to you?"*

Relax, and listen. Suppose they reply with a comment about seeing to her education. You reset the stage and continue. *"Education may mean one thing to one family and quite something else to another, so tell me, what's important about her guardian seeing to her education to you?"*

Mom replies that she has a dream of her daughter attending the same college that she did. Write it down. You reset the stage and ask the reformulated *"WIA attending Alma Mater University TY"* question. This time, the answer focuses on having funds on hand when needed for college. Write it down, and ask, *"WIA having funds on hand for college TY"?* The reply indicates a desire that their daughter have get a good start in life. Write it down, and then again ask, *"WIA her achieving her full potential and getting a good start in life TY?"*

In their reply, Dad states that this is how they see their responsibility as parents of bringing a new life into the world, and they want to assure that if they were gone, they had made arrangements that would fulfill that responsibility.

You ask the Confirming Question, *"Is there anything more important to you than making arrangements that fulfill your responsibility as parents to give your daughter an education and a good start in life?"*

If the answer is no, you are at the top floor. Ask for a Pre-commitment. *"Suppose we could create a plan so that you would name a guardian, who, if the need arose, would see to your daughter's education and the plan would also contain arrangements to guarantee that the money necessary to pay for her education and give her a start in life would be there, to enable you to feel that you had fulfilled your responsibility as parents? If that were the case, would that be a basis for us to work together?"*

If yes, then you are ready for a transition, into thorough fact-finding, discussing the steps of selecting a guardian, the advisability of creating a trust in the Will, and the various ways to fund it. The *Values Conversation* opens up the opportunity to do more work than just a simple Will to name a guardian. It provides a basis for the work to be powerfully justified and highly valued in the clients' minds because of the powerful benefits being provided that directly fulfill a core value.

Engaging clients in conversations about values provides information so you can understand how your services will benefit the client. It sets the emotional stage for your client's acceptance and satisfaction from the very best services you have to offer. And the conversation itself motivates clients to chose the best solutions and not settle for what little they knew when they first came in to see you. Clients willingly "upsell" themselves your *Success Solution.*

Tips to Improve Your Listening

When you are engaging in these new styles, you may feel awkward at first. But do not let that prevent from trying out these tools. They work. After you modify them a bit to fit yourself better, they will work even better. There is always room for improving communications. Here are some other tips.

- Of the time spent with the client, spend less than half of it with you yourself talking.

- Ask more questions. Listen, restate what you heard, get affirmation, then write down your notes.

- Eliminate habits that interfere with listening. Have a staff member sit in and observe nervous mannerisms, gestures or facial expressions, other non-verbal indicators that you are not listening.

- Break the mental habit of trying to impress, of always figuring out what you are going to say next. Such distraction from the present increases the potential for unarticulated misunderstanding.

- Listen intently to the speaker, and make no judgment. Focus on understanding the speakers' point of view. Suspend your evaluation and analytical thoughts. While difficult for lawyers, by giving your total attention to your client's message, emotion and intent, you impart greater depth to your professional relationship. You also let your clients know that what they are telling you is really being absorbed.

- Practice with nonjudgmental phrases like *"go on"* or *"oh?"* to invite more, and to keep the flow of communication coming.

- Spend the time to explore the clients' values around the issues under discussion, and make them part of the *Success Solution*.

These techniques open the door to developing legal services that really satisfy clients' needs, both objective and emotional. Clients decide to engage you to provide a higher level of service and decide that it is worthwhile to pay you a higher fee, based on the objective and emotional perception of a higher level of benefit.

Afterwards, they seek through reason to have a rationale that they really have done the very best. This is because a perception of value is subjective, and may even be more emotional than rational. Using the techniques discussed in this Chapter will bring amazing changes in the way that clients relate to you.

Your Notes

Chapter Seven:
The Happy Lawyer's Practice

Happy are they whose natures sort with their vocations.
— Francis Bacon

Congratulations! You are on your way! Look at all you have covered.

- You have dug up the *Seeds of Satisfaction* in your practice.

- You have thought about and defined your *Practice Purpose.*

- You have explored whom you wish to serve, and have profiled your *YES! Clients.*

- You can articulate in a compelling *Spoken Logo* the powerful benefits clients can receive only by working with you, in your *Arena of Preeminence.*

- You have learned *Breakthrough Communications* techniques that engender deep trust with clients. You can demonstrate a real interest in clients and their values, something that will leave most clients astonished.

The Happy Lawyer provide clients something that they cannot get anywhere else —*YOU!*

Your action plan gives you specific steps to take in the coming days. Yet, no single program will instantaneously transform your present situation into your ideal practice. It will take dedicated effort — inspired by the work we have done together.

Ready, Fire, Aim!

Take action now! Only by taking action will you make progress towards achieving your goals. But the path you follow may not always be straight. It may more closely resemble the flight of a guided missile. First, prepare. Then, launch. Finally, make course corrections as you go. That is why the sequence of your steps is *"Ready, fire, aim!"*

You *practice* law, you do not master it. So, too, is becoming *The Happy Lawyer* a matter of practice. The process set out in this book has been one of discovery, decision, focus, attraction, communications, service, and fulfillment.

As lawyers, whether we win or lose cases, and regardless of how much money we may or may not make, we can learn to enjoy practicing law, and we can become better at what we do by changing how we think.

You can control how you project yourself. You can dig down deep, and find out what it is that makes you the happiest and what you have passion about.

As one of the lawyers in my teleclasses observed, "When I'm acting on my mission, I enjoy the law." In your *Happy Lawyer* practice, focus on those clients, those cases, and those services you truly enjoy. Then take action to be sure you do not remain mired in a field that does not inspire you.

With your best field and best work in hand, you determine for whom you want to work. Who are your *YES! clients*? Where is your passion for your *Practice Purpose*? That work will bring out the very best in you. And you can count on a deeper sustained joy in your work than you have ever allowed yourself to have.

Use the marketing principles we have discussed. Position yourself in the market. Aim your marketing message directly at the prospective *YES! Clients* out there. When you receive the chance to work with one, be enthusiastic and demonstrate to them the powerful benefits your services offer them. Practice *active listening*. Reflect what clients they tell you, and its importance to them. Show them goals and objectives responsive to what their communications tell you about their values and desires.

Explain how your services satisfy their goals and objectives, and seek their agreement. They will enjoy deep satisfaction, too, in feeling they have been heard and are cared about. In turn, these connections will support your premium fee request. Clients will happily pay you the value of what you are doing to create and deliver their *Success Solution*.

Build on this. Remind clients of their satisfaction, and *ask for referrals* to other people like them whom they know might also benefit from what you do. Your practice will grow. You will probably earn more money while working fewer hours. Most importantly, you will be doing work that satisfies you at your deepest level. This is the satisfying and prosperous *Happy Lawyer* practice.

Your Notes

Additional Sources

Introduction

Dissatisfaction reported in *The State of the Legal Profession* (American Bar Association, 1991)

Attorneys and depression from Eaton, et al., "Occupations and the Prevalence of Major Depressive Disorder," 32 *Journal of Occupational Medicine*, No. 11, 1083-85 (1990)

Disliked clients or work percentages from David H. Maister, *True Professionalism: The Courage to Care About Your People, Your Clients, and Your Career* (Free Press, 1997)

Unhappiness of sole practitioners reported in "Sole Practitioners Among the Unhappy," *National Law Journal*, May 28, 1990.

Professional satisfaction as a lawyering skill from Daniel B. Evans, "Unlearning Dissatisfaction," *Lawyering Skills Bulletin*, Vol. 6, No. 2 (Winter 1996)

Chapter One

Four fundamental values from the "MacCrate Report" *Legal Education and Professional Development: An Educational Continuum* (American Bar Association, 1992)

Gerry Spence, *Gunning for Justice: My Life and Trials*, (Doubleday, 1982)

Career choices and self-image from Super & Crites, *Appraising Vocational Fitness* (Harper and Row, 1962)

"Tough-minded, bottom-line decision makers and conceptual complex problem solvers" characterization of lawyers from Byers, "Career Choice & Satisfaction in the Legal Profession," *Career Planning & Adult Development Journal*, Spring 1996

"Avoidance of involvement at the heart of the lawyer's dilemma" from Benjamin Sells, *The Soul of the Law*, 112 (Element Books, 1994)

Chapter Two

Percentages of clients or work disliked from Maister, *supra*

Chapter Four

Fee guarantee quotation from Maister, *supra*.

Sole practitioner's experience reported in "Offer Your Clients a Money-Back Guarantee," *Lawyers Weekly USA*, July 28, 1997

Chapter Five

Action steps to more referrals based on David M. Ward, Esq., *Referral Magic: The Complete Guide to Attracting New Clients and*

Developing a Successful Law Practice! (Golden Lantern Publications, 1997). Used with permission.

Chapter Six

Ineffective listeners characterized as "boorish, self-centered, disinterested, preoccupied and socially unacceptable" and the five factors contributing to poor listening from Dr. Tony Alessandra, *Communicating at Work*, (Simon & Schuster, 1993). Used with permission.

Active listening and reflecting resources found in Goodman, *The Talk Book: The Intimate Science of Communicating in Close Relationships* (Ballantine, 1988) and Binder, et al., *Lawyers As Counselors: A Client-Centered Approach*, (West, 1991).

The values conversation and values elevator are concepts based on Bill Bachrach's *Values-Based Selling: The Art of High-Trust Client Relationships for Financial Advisors, Insurance Agents and Investment Reps*, (Aim High, 1996). Used with permission.

Appendix
Worksheets

No. 1:   Remembering

No. 2:   Heroes

No. 3:   Aspirations

No. 4:   Being in The "Flow"

No. 5:   My Beliefs About Lawyers

No. 6:   Discover Your *Yes! Clients*

No. 7:   Focusing On Satisfaction

No. 8:   Telescoping

No. 9:   Delegation

No. 10:   Differentiating Yourself

No. 11:   Writing an Article the Easy Way

No. 12:   Your Potential Allies

Worksheet No. 1: Remembering

- Put aside for a moment the concerns of the present day, and let your mind relax. Read each of the following, close your eyes, and call to mind whatever images, feelings, memories, people, situations, they evoke. After brief reflection on each one, jot down a note or two.

A. Call to mind the earliest occasion you can recall when you started considering becoming a lawyer. What particular person, event, or cause was involved?

_____

B. If you had other alternatives under consideration, what were they? What factors led you to choose the path you did?

_____

C. If ever you thought of quitting either law school or law practice, what considerations were you weighing at that time?

_____

D. You have remained with the law. Jot down a few words or phrases that indicate the factors that influenced you to stick with it.

_____

A. Call to mind all your work experiences, volunteer positions, summer jobs, or other employment completed before entering law. Of those that had any bearing on your career choice, jot down the images, feelings, or memories that they invoke.

_____

_____

B. List all the skills you employed in these positions, and any key talents you possessed that were either key to your success or were left unused.

_____

_____

_____

Worksheet No. 2: Heroes

A. Name three people whom you'd call your heroes, whether known
    to you personally, historical figures, or familial ancestors.

    _____

B. For the three heroes you named, write several phrases or words
    that capture the characteristic quality that makes this person a
    hero. A list of traits or characteristics to aid you with your heroes
    is found on Page 37.

    _____

C. Write down the primary trait or characteristic you find yourself
    drawn to: _____

D. To emulate this trait or characteristic more fully in your law
    practice, what would you have to change?

    _____

Worksheet No. 3: Aspirations

Complete the following sentences:

A. When I was in junior or senior high school, my most exciting daydream about my future was:

_____

B. My favorite paid jobs before entering law were:

_____

C. When I started law school, I saw the future as:

_____

D. If I had all the financial security I need and I knew I could not fail, I would spend most of my time involved in:

_____

Worksheet No. 4: Being in The "Flow"

- Sit quietly for a moment. Close your eyes if it helps you to concentrate.

- See yourself engaged in your practice, in your office, in court, at a client's, or elsewhere. What are you doing? Are you standing or sitting? Talking or listening? Writing or reading?

- Now bring to mind an instance you remember where you found that you had become so engrossed in your work, that you lost track of the time. As soon as you have a clear instance, begin the worksheet.

Three absorbing activities in my practice:

_____

_____

What I enjoy the most about the activity:

_____

Specific skills I employ when I am "in the flow":

_____

Worksheet No. 5: My Beliefs About Lawyers

"I believe these negative stereotypes of lawyers are mostly *true*:

_____

_____

_____

"I believe these negative stereotypes of lawyers are mostly *false*:

_____

_____

_____

"Three *strongly positive things* I can say about lawyers, in my experience, are:

_____

_____

_____

Worksheet No. 6 : Discover Your *Yes! Clients*

A. Gather together your past year or two years' client list, case list, pocket organizer and calendar, any other compilations that will assist you bring to mind those with whom you have been working. Then complete the following worksheet, ranking each entry from 1 to 3, assigning 1 to clients you most enjoyed working with, and 3 to those that you would rather have go elsewhere. (Use extra sheets as necessary.)

Client Name	Ranking Enjoy(ed) =1 Take-or-leave =2 Go away! = 3	Type of Matter	Ranking Enjoy(ed) =1 Take-or-leave =2 Go away! = 3

B.   Next, go over the results. For each client you ranked a one, write down the particular issue or problem that you worked on and how you resolved it for them. Spell out in specific detail what the problem was, what the work entailed and how your efforts provided a satisfying solution to the client's problem.

<u>Client Name</u> <u>Issue</u> <u>**What I Did to Address Problem**</u>

_____

_____

_____

_____

_____

C.   Now it is time to pull out the nuggets. Look over the clients you have listed. For each one, reflect on what it was about that particular client that appealed to you. What were they like? What was their personality like? What was your working relationship like? What characteristics are recurring among those clients on your list? Jot them down:

_____

_____

_____

D. Now, how about the particular matters. Were there recurring kinds of issues, problems, or legal processes involved? Do some projects call upon your special strength in one or another field? What about the work strongly appeals to you? Jot those down:

_____

_____

_____

_____

E. Finally, what skills and particular knowledge are you called upon to employ in addressing these problems?

_____

_____

F. Now, look for the values, the emerging common themes, activities, skills, knowledge, in your favored clients, problems, projects, and solutions. List the common or overlapping themes:

_____

_____

Worksheet No. 7: Focusing On Satisfaction

A.   Three Aspects of My Practice That Really Hold My Interest:

1. _____

2. _____

3. _____

B.   Three Skills or Talents Used in My Practice At Which I Excel:

1. _____

2. _____

3. _____

C.   Three Values of Importance to Me I Would Like My Practice to Serve:

1. _____

2. _____

3. _____

D.   Next, in the following table, match up each possible pair from the nine Aspects, Skills, and Values you filled in above. With each match, what relationship do they have? What sort of connection occurs to you? How might each pair relate? Jot down a word or two describing the relationship or connection.

	Aspect 1	Aspect 2	Aspect 3	Skill 1	Skill 2	Skill 3	Value 1	Value 2	Value 3
Aspect 1									
Aspect 2									
Aspect 3									
Skill 1									
Skill 2									
Skill 3									
Value 1									
Value 2									
Value 3									

E.   Of all the connections and relationships, which two or three attract you the most? If you could implant those into your daily work in the practice of law, which would you choose to concentrate upon?

Worksheet No. 8: Telescoping

A. *If you knew you could not fail* and you were assured absolutely everything you wanted, in the way of time, resources, talent, and energy, *what would you choose to do in your profession?*

_____

_____

B. *How much free time* to spend as you choose (family, hobbies, service, recreation, travel) do you want in the next year? Per week? Per month?

_____

_____

C. *How much money* do you want to make as a result of spending your working time on work? Per week? Per month? Per year?

_____

D. *What solutions to your YES! Client's problems can you provide* in a cost effective way?

_____

E. Which *YES! clients* you now have and prospects you've identified, *what work can you do to give them so much value that they will pay you the fee income necessary* to earn your goal level?

_____

Worksheet No. 9: Delegation

A. Among all the activities that make up your practice day, what activities and tasks truly require that only you do them?:

_____

B. Now take a closer look. How many of those activities and tasks could you train someone to do as well as you? List everything that an assistant or other staff member can do:

_____

_____

C. What sort of delegation plan can you devise to free up time to spend on what only you can do? Lay out in a flowchart, grid, list, or however you like, how work might better flow. Take a sample project and map out all the steps.

PROJECT:

Step No. ____:

Who Could Do This:

Project activities & tasks that could be delegated to a staff member are:

_____

Worksheet No. 10: Differentiating Yourself

Differentiation is making yourself stand out from the others in a positive light. This worksheet will help you to do that for yourself and your practice.

A. List quickly, with minimum analysis, your characteristics which you feel make you different from your competitors.

1. The special qualities in what I provide my clients that are not routinely done by other lawyers are: _____

2. I am unique in my field because: _____

3. My uniqueness is enhanced by these qualifications and experiences:

_____

B. Re-state your uniqueness as a client-benefits statement:

The benefits my clients uniquely receive are: _____

_____

C. What particularly differentiates my services I would describe as:

_____

Worksheet No. 11: Writing an Article the Easy Way

A.   Pick your topic. _____

B.   In 30 seconds, jot down all the key words or concepts you can, with only minimal detail or elaboration.

_____

_____

C.   Now group the concepts or key words into 3 points you will make.

_____

D.   Under each key point, write a sentence for each phrase or key word.

E.   Cut and paste the text until it flows logically and smoothly.

F.   Add a three-sentence introductory paragraph: 1. state the problem or topic; 2. suggest the answer; 3. state that you will explain.

G.   Add a brief conclusion that mirrors the introductory paragraph: 1. restate the problem or topic; 2. tick off in summary fashion the answers; 3. state the actions your conclusion suggest will benefit the reader.

Worksheet No. 12: Your Potential Allies

A. List 10 non-competitor contacts whose clients fit your *YES!* Clients

1. _____   6. _____

2. _____   7. _____

3. _____   8. _____

4. _____   9. _____

5. _____   10. _____

B. Describe the benefits you could provide to these clients.

_____

C. What information do your contacts need to have to enable them to convey your benefits to their clients? A "special report," a "resources guide," reprints of articles, a book or audiotape? Brainstorm. Come up with 3. Jot down several phrases describing the benefits for their clients.

_____

D. Write a letter to your contacts, presenting these ideas and potential benefits to them and their clients. Ask to meet with them to discuss and get their reactions and suggestions. Send out and follow up with phone or personal contacts.

Index

Order Form

FAX orders: (253)850-1549
Telephone orders: Toll Free: 1(888)707-5397. VISA or MasterCard.
Internet orders: http://www.happylawyer.com
E-mail orders: sales@shilohpub.com
Postal orders: Shiloh Publications
                    24909 104th Ave. SE., Suite 204
                    Kent, WA 98031 USA
                    Tel. (253)850-1551

Please send me _____ copies of *The Happy Lawyer* @ $39.95 per book.

Name _____
Street Address _____
City: _____ State: _____ Zip:_____
Telephone: (____) _____

Sales Tax: Please add 8.6% for books shipped to Washington addresses.
Shipping: $3 per book (1-10 books); over 10 books, 10% of total order.
Method of Payment:
○ Check or Money Order (US$ Only) payable to Shiloh Publications

○ Credit card: ○ VISA   ○ MasterCard
Card number: _____ Exp. Date: ____/____
Name on card: _____
Signature: _____

Call *toll free* and order now